DIVINE GUIDANCE

Divine Guidance

Seeking to Find and Follow the Will of God

SUSAN MUTO
AND ADRIAN VAN KAAM

CHARIS

Servant Publications
Ann Arbor, Michigan

Scripture selections are taken from the *New American Bible*. Wichita, KS:
Catholic Bible Publishers, 1992-93 edition.

Imprimatur: Most Reverend Donald William Wuerl
　　　　　　　Bishop of Pittsburgh
　　　　　　　August 1, 1994

The Nihil obstat and the imprimatur are declarations that this work is
considered to be free from doctrinal or moral error. It is not implied that
those who have granted the same agree with the contents, opinion, or
statements expressed.

Charis Books is an imprint of Servant Publications especially designed to
serve Roman Catholics.

Published by Servant Publications
P.O. Box 8617
Ann Arbor, Michigan 48107

Cover design by Paula Murphy, Hile Design and Illustration

95 96 97 98 10 9 8 7 6 5 4 3 2

Printed in the United States of America
ISBN 0-89283-857-4

Library of Congress Cataloging-in-Publication Data

Muto, Susan Annette.
Divine guidance : seeking to find and follow the will of God /
Susan Muto and Adrian van Kaam.
　　pm.　cm.
includes bibliographical references.
ISBN 0-89283-857-4
1. Providence and government of God.　2. God—Will.　3.
Christian life—Catholic authors.　I. van Kaam, Adrian L., 1920-
.　II. Title.
BX2350.7.M88　1994
248.2–dc20
　　　　　　　　　　　　　　　　　　　　94-22690
　　　　　　　　　　　　　　　　　　　　CIP

Divine Guidance
Adrian van Kaam

Splendor of the Trinity,
Sprouting tenderly the mighty tree
Of God's Eternal Word,
In whom are stored silent seeds
Soon to be twigs and branches
Rustling as the Spirit dances
In the foliage of their leaves.

Dawn of holy light,
Mirror of splendor bright,
We are your princely people,
Begotten in the Word,
Dwelling in the court
Of Majesty: interforming "We"
Of Blessed Trinity
Whose dance we share adoptively.

Let us dance with Thee delightedly
In spite of traces in heart and faces
Of bygone days and wounded ways.
Break in upon us, lovely Light,
Lift us beyond the blight
Dense and dim as endless night.

Guide our dirty feet
Treading slushy roads and streets
Into your shiny paths of peace.
Grant us your Spirit,
Luminous key to guidance divine
Piercing the specter of time.

Contents

Acknowledgments

We would like to acknowledge the invaluable help we received in preparing this manuscript from our typist, Mary Lou Perez.

We also want to thank our staff at the Epiphany Association for their support of this work, naming with special gratitude our administrative assistant, Marilyn Russell.

We are grateful as well for the faithful audience who came to our Monday evening Ongoing Formation Sessions at the Kelly House where many of these ideas on faith deepening and divine guidance were first presented.

We offer words of heartfelt thanks to David Came of Servant Publications, who invited us to write this book, and to Heidi Hess, our editor, who helped us in a diligent and expert way to bring it to completion.

CHAPTER ONE

The Mystery of Divine Guidance

You have been endowed from your birth with princely gifts; in eternal splendor, before the dawn of life on earth, I have begotten you. **Advent Antiphon**

"Princely gifts!" What might they be? How can I discover this royal inheritance? How can I find and follow the right path in decisions large and small?

Is there any way I can be sure that I am abandoning my life to God's guidance and not just listening to the voice of my own willfulness? How do I know if I am listening to the Holy Spirit when I choose to marry or remain single, to pursue a career or to work at home? If I am flowing with or resisting the call to follow Christ as a priest, brother, sister, minister, or lay person?

When all is said and done, what is God's will for my life? Whether a homemaker, parent, laborer, executive, or teacher, how can I be sure if I am living in fidelity to the Divine Will? When do I need to surrender in faith to what is unseen, yet still believed?

Such profound questions can haunt all of us who sincerely try to follow in the footsteps of Christ. We want to understand more about how God communicates with us. We want to be able to recognize in our everyday lives certain pointers that can provide sound direction. In short, we want to find and follow God's will for our lives.

Yet our sincere search for divine guidance inevitably brings us to the threshold of a profound mystery that no one can penetrate entirely. We can only try to place our questions in the context of deepening faith, hope, and love. Faith that the Father will show us the way. Hope that the Son will bless our search. Love for the Holy Spirit who guides our best efforts.

We have written this book with two main objectives in mind. Our first goal is to help you more clearly *find* God's will for your life. To the degree that you are growing in obedient discipleship, this will happen. Our second goal is to suggest a number of practical ways in which you can *follow* the indicators of divine guidance in actually living out your call and vocation. This can be even trickier.

What we cannot offer you are "Ten Easy Steps" to complete certitude that you are fulfilling the divine plan for your life. Facile solutions to finding and following God's will often result in either superficiality ("The Holy Spirit told me...") or self-centeredness ("I *know* God wants me to...").

In all honesty, we will struggle over a lifetime to hear the Father's call to us in Christ. The Holy Spirit—who is likened to the wind that blows where it will (Jn 3:8)—often inspires us in ways that are not easy to find or follow. Pitfalls await us at every turn of the road, not the least of which are temptation and sin, demonic seduction and self-deception, rationalization and complacency.

Many other dangers await us. We may be unwilling to endure the night of faith, those times when the guiding light of God seems to fade from our sight. The illusion of perfectionism may seriously detour our journey to divine union. To feel perfectly sure that "now I have made it" or that "now I am absolutely guided by God" is to risk being swallowed by the quicksand of pride.

Despite all these pitfalls and perils, God promises to guide us. In straight or winding pathways, in the brightness of day or the darkness of night, the Father who loves us promises to lead us home.

Thankfully, we don't have to rely on our own meager resources. The one who calls us is faithful, and he will do it (1 Thes 5:24).

WHAT DOES THE "WILL OF GOD" MEAN?

To find, to follow, and to be faithful to God's will implies that we know what the "will of God" means. Let us be clear about one thing: it does not refer to a precise blueprint drawn by the "Great Architect in the sky." Some people harbor the dubious notion of God's will as a preconceived plan demanding strict conformity to every detail.

A more accurate image compares the divine will to a call from a close friend. It is at once inviting, appealing, and challenging. It leaves room for free choice: We can resist or refuse this call or give our willing consent. The call comes to us and we have to respond.

When we feel uncertain of our life direction, we must not expect to find a secret "red phone"—as if we could dial an 800-number and hear a booming voice declare that this or that is the right way to go. Just as there are no "Ten Easy Steps" to certitude, so there is no "Hot Line to Heaven."

A better way to define God's will is by relating it to the *universal call to holiness.* Only in following the call to imitate Christ can we begin to know the divine will. As we focus on Christ, we can approximate with deepening fidelity its specifics, say in relation to our choice of vocation (married or single) or profession (typographer or teacher). As we grow in holiness, we may find ourselves seeking to follow the divine will in simpler matters like how to dress or decorate our home, where to spend our summer vacation, what guests we want to entertain this Friday evening.

Finding, following, and being faithful to the call of God eventually form the all-encompassing horizon against which we view our daily lives. Mature Christians do not wait for spectacular instances of divine intervention—like the most glorious sunrise or sunset over the bluest ocean. Rather they seek the Lord in their everydayness, in the ordinary, often barely perceptible inspirations of the Holy Spirit. They learn to depend on their Divine Caller to guide them each step of the way, however mundane.

All of us need spend only a few minutes looking back over the years to realize how much we have already been led by God. If we have managed to make something beautiful of our daily existence, it is because the Holy Spirit has been hovering over us. In the words of the psalmist: "I will remember you upon my couch, and through the night-watches I will meditate on you: that you are my help, and in the shadow of your wings I shout for joy" (Ps 63:7-8).

Writing this book has made us more aware of the protective role God's guiding will has played in our own lives. Before we go on to present the principles of divine guidance, we would like to share with you a few instances of this mystery in our own journey of faith and formation. These stories will help you to know us more personally, and to realize that we are fellow pilgrims often groping to find the obscure pathway ahead, just like you.

THE LITTLE DUTCH BOY:
HIGHLIGHTS FROM FR. ADRIAN'S STORY

I was born in 1920 in the Hague, the seat of government in my native country of Holland. When I was nine years old, divine guidance led my devout parents to subscribe to a Dutch youth journal called *Het Missie Vriendje*, which means "The Little Friend of the Missions." Fr. Jan van der Zandt, more familiarly known as "Uncle John," wrote a correspondence column to his young readers. The Spirit moved me to write to this priest regularly. I both enjoyed and obeyed his printed answers. In hindsight I realize that his replies sounded a lot like spiritual guidance.

When the end of my elementary school education drew near, "Uncle John" surprised us with a handwritten letter that was to set my whole life on a new course. He felt from my letters that God was guiding me to become a priest, and invited me to join the junior seminary of the Spiritan fathers. Perceiving the hand of God, I and my parents felt that we should gladly obey this directive, no matter what sacrifices it asked of us.

My friend Rinus. Another disclosure of the Divine Will awaited me at the junior seminary, where God began to speak to me through a specially graced friend, Marinus Scholtes. In the Hague, his parents lived in a parish neighboring that of my own family. Rinus was already fourteen, two years ahead of me in the junior seminary.

As we matured and grew closer as friends, we shared a common desire to delve into the mystery of God's guidance in our lives. We asked ourselves how we could grow together in obedience to divine inspirations. I watched Rinus change, especially toward the end of his six years at the high school. He seemed blessed with mysterious graces as he became more and more at one with Christ by his everyday obedience to the transforming guidance of the Holy Spirit.

My friend went on to enter the novitiate of the Spiritans, where divine guidance continued to manifest itself in extraordinary graces. The Holy Spirit seemed to draw Rinus into contemplative union with the Holy Trinity. I later learned that this union, referred to as "mystical marriage" by the spiritual masters, is God's crowning gift of a believer's spiritual journey.

I myself was far less advanced than Rinus on the path of obedient simplicity. I also found it difficult to believe that my simple, childlike friend could have been chosen at such an early age for these extraordinary graces. When I entered the same novitiate two years later, I asked the novice master, Fr. Joseph Strick, about my friend's exemplary life.

Using the French word *candeur*, or "candor" in English, he explained that the Holy Spirit often guides people to unusual holiness in plain and common ways. Their comings and goings may not be at all remarkable in a worldly sense. Yet their childlike obedience gives them a glow of candor: simplicity and openness to the grace of God. These graced believers are found not only inside seminaries and religious communities but also in our everyday world. The Spirit sanctifies them through obedience to God's guidance as it becomes known to them in the simple tasks and struggles of daily life.

Three years later, at the age of twenty-two, Rinus became terribly ill from consumption. In the last weeks before his death, God used him again and again as a channel of wisdom for my own life. After answering his call to be with him in his final moments, I watched my friend die.

Before his final hour, Rinus told me repeatedly of his conviction that God had given him the gift of our spiritual friendship for a good reason: to prepare me for the message of obedience to God's guidance in every human life, no matter how simple and common that life may be. And he assured me that he would continue to help me in my task even after he had passed on to a better life.

The war years. I experienced the grace of God's guiding presence some years later when I was in hiding during the last year of World War II. As a priest, I had to sustain the famined, bereft, and anxious people around me in the Dutch Hunger Winter of 1944-1945. I tried to encourage them to grow in obedient faith to God's guidance, even in the midst of suffering, starvation, and terrifying uncertainty.

In the aftermath of the war, I was asked to do the same for young mill workers. Concerned that low morale could seriously affect the output of their impoverished laborers, the mill bosses set aside a few hours each week for inspirational talks in factory cafeterias. As these spiritually hungry people gathered around me, my task as their teacher was to impart strength during trying times.

Later, sent to America by my community, I was asked to teach and initiate a program of psychology. This confusing detour lasted nine years, during which I had to postpone the formation work I had started in Holland. I went through a period when I seemed unable to listen fully to God's guidance—not that I wasn't trying.

I vividly remember a surprising reminder from the Holy Spirit that I might be losing the way God intended for me. As a speaker to a small group at a large retreat center, I had heard some rumors about a woman in another group who had unexpectedly changed from a worldly life to a life of prayer. She fasted, spent hours in the chapel, and surprised everyone in her Bible study group by her deep insights into their texts—even though she had never done any formal Scripture study.

Being busy with my own work, I didn't pay much attention to this story. Then one evening, while I was relaxing in my room, I heard a timid knock on my door. I opened it to find a hesitant lady who profusely apologized for disturbing me. She said, "I do not know the meaning of what I have been asked to tell you. It makes no sense to me at all. I was praying for hours in the chapel when suddenly I heard a clear, inner voice, such as I had never heard before. It told me repeatedly to go to the Father in the guest room and say, 'If you keep excusing yourself, you may get lost.'"

I told her that the words did not make sense to me either, and asked her to return to her room or the chapel. The woman left immediately, relieved that I hadn't scolded her or made fun of her message. But her words did not leave me. Instead, they began to burn in my heart like fire.

I do not know whether or not God had really spoken to me through this woman. What I do know is that divine guidance began to use these words to make me aware of a dangerous drift: *I was beginning to be less obedient to God's mission for my life.* The Holy Spirit cautioned me gently that disobedience to his guidance, in spite of my clever excuses, could result in losing the real mission God intended for me. For example, one excuse I used was that teaching at the university made it impossible to invest more time in my original call to serve the spiritual formation of people by writing and public speaking.

I could share many more incidents of divine guidance in my life, along with ample evidence of the tension between obedience and disobedience. I hope these few events will help to explain why the topic of divine guidance has such a strong hold on me.

BEGINNINGS AND ENDINGS:
HIGHLIGHTS FROM SUSAN'S STORY

I was born in Pittsburgh in 1942, the eldest of three children, two brothers and myself. My father had immigrated to America from southern Italy with his parents when he was six years old. My mother was born and raised in an Italian Catholic family as well.

I have no doubt that both my parents exerted a strong influence on my life from its earliest days. Later I would learn that what we believe (our *faith* tradition) and how we live it every day (our *formation* tradition) must commingle if we are to be obedient to God's loving and guiding will. This vital link was at the root of a theology of formation. Little did I know at the time that Fr. Adrian was already well on the way to articulating this approach to life in the Lord, and that our paths were destined to cross.

Without mitigating the usual growing pains, I can say that I had a healthy, happy childhood surrounded by people with a zest for life, a love for good food, and a strong conviction that God was a friend on whom we could depend for help and guidance in times that were tough or splendid. The greatest influence on my childhood faith was my maternal grandmother Elizabeth, my "Nunny." She and my grandfather lived across the street from us. I knew her for only the first thirteen years of my life, but her confidence in God still provides a pillar of strength for me whenever I'm tempted to doubt.

When Nunny first moved into the house across the street from us, she had to put up with neighbors who laughed when she said she would soon have a huge vegetable garden. They assured her that nothing would grow in the mostly clay soil there, and that she might as well find another hobby since gardening was out of the question.

Little did they know the link between my grandmother and God. Not only did she have a "green thumb" but she also had the faith of a peasant, a childlike faith at once trusting and wise like the candor of Fr. Adrian's friend, Rinus. I feel certain that if my grandmother opened the back door and said, "Excuse me, Lord, that mountain is in my way," God would have replied, "No problem, Elizabeth. For you, I'll move it."

Within a year Nunny was delivering vegetables to the neighbors, along with loaves of fresh bread and bottles of my grandfather's prize-winning wine (whenever he gave his permission, of course).

I knew that my grandmother had terminal stomach cancer, but the finality of her illness never fully registered until my mother told me to prepare myself for Nunny's passage to heaven. I was thirteen years old at the time. I prayed with the passion only a child can muster that she would recover, but every time I saw her I could tell the light was growing dim. Not even the full force of my love could push away the determined force of death.

With the passing of the years, I have come to see how God guided me and my vocation as a teacher and spiritual writer through Nunny's faith-filled witness of his steadfast love. She had accepted God's plan for her life in the face of almost insurmountable odds. At the age of sixteen, my grandmother had traveled by steamer from southern Italy to America to marry a man she had met only briefly through a matchmaker. Of her eleven children, five died before puberty, some in childbirth.

Nunny enjoyed few times of peace and prosperity during her seventy-two years, but she never complained. In her heart she believed God had reasons that reason itself could never grasp. This illiterate but brilliant woman of wisdom taught me many lasting lessons. Having witnessed the depths of her faith and its power to sustain her throughout an excruciating illness, I could no longer deny the likelihood of a divine design for my life as well.

Because Nunny had trusted God's love, even when she was alone and in pain, I determined to do the same. My resolution to emulate my grandmother was no bigger than a mustard seed, but her life remains the remembered soil in which my faith continues to grow.

A backyard bout with God. A few months after this loss, I had my first major fight with God (an indicator, no doubt, of the slow-as-a-turtle pace of my own spiritual progress). During one of the many hours I spent alone in my room daydreaming, reading, and just missing Nunny, I began voicing this vague promise to live my life in tune with the forming power on which she had based her faith. What I was not prepared to accept were the demands such an assent might mean.

To all outward appearances I was pretty and popular, but in my heart I knew I was being prompted to another level of awareness. But of what? Of whom? I wondered if others my age ever thought as much about life and death as I did. I found no clear answers in my religion classes, nor did I feel called to the convent as did some of the girls in my Catholic school.

One day I decided to have it out with God. I vented my anger and confusion. I wanted him to either answer the great questions or leave me alone. I wanted out of the pact I had made at the time of my grandmother's death, the promise to be faithful—whatever that might mean. I was suffering the pains of inner solitude, pretending to conform to peer notions of fun when I really felt fragmented. I was conscious of being beckoned to I knew not where, and I was afraid.

I remember walking to the end of our yard and begging God to let me be like everyone else. I didn't want to take the road less traveled or dance to a different drummer. When the venting ceased, I felt drained of emotion but strangely at peace. It was as if God had confirmed my feelings by allowing me to be exactly who and where I was.

The meaning of these two events, Nunny's death and my backyard bout with God, have never left me. They formed a foundation for my life of faith, and in one way or another disclosed a pattern for my life of prayer. When I am at my lowest ebb, and yet perfectly honest with God, the gloom lessens and a new direction is delicately disclosed. Bits and pieces of my early and later formation gather around these seminal events of birth and death, beginnings and endings, goals reached and uncharted terrain yet to traverse.

Crossing paths with Fr. Adrian. After high school and college, where I majored in English literature and journalism, I felt my destiny lay in the editorial field. God clearly had another plan. While successful in my career, I was not happy. So I made the "mistake" of praying with the faith of a peasant, as Nunny had taught me.

My words must have been heard because within months I met Fr. Adrian van Kaam. I soon joined him and some other colleagues in establishing the Institute of Formative Spirituality at Duquesne University, a new graduate school program which he had begun to develop a few years earlier. I completed my Ph.D. at the University of Pittsburgh, with a specialty in the literature of post-reformation spirituality.

I spent the next several years teaching at the Institute while I continued editing our journals and writing a number of books on the art and discipline of formative reading of Scripture and the masters. My teaching and administrative career at the Institute ended up spanning over twenty years; I succeeded Fr. Adrian as director in 1980.

My work then took an unexpected turn in 1988. After a long period of appraisal, I somehow knew that God was calling me to resign my university position and move into full-time ministry in the field of lay formation. It was not that I heard a direct voice—no such luck! In fact, by the world's standards, I as a single woman seemed to be giving up a lot of security.

Family members and colleagues expressed concerns of the "you-must-be-kidding" variety. I myself experienced the usual flutters of uncertainty that surround any major life decision. Nonetheless, all of my reading, study, and consultation with others assured me that I was hearing the Lord. The inner peace and joy I felt when I assented to divine guidance offered certitude enough to make my move.

In response to divine guidance, I became the executive director of the Epiphany Association, a nonprofit ecumenical center I had cofounded with Fr. Adrian and others of like-minded dedication in 1979. I pledged to devote myself to its aims of research, publication, education, consultation, and resource development in the field of human and Christian formation.

Both Fr. Adrian and I attribute the primary influence in our life direction at this time to our providential meeting with a new friend and colleague. In 1982, we began a graced friendship with Dr. George Armstrong Kelly, IV, a professor of political philosophy and religion at Johns Hopkins University. This man of simple tastes and profound faith became our principal benefactor by donating his family home, the Kelly House in Pittsburgh, to our fledgling group.

George's unprecedented gift provided a sign of confirmation like no other we have ever received. It is in this lovely old Victorian setting that the Epiphany Association is presently headquartered. We strive with the help of many others to meet a growing need for adult Christian formation in the modern world, both in family life and in the marketplace.

I identified with these women and men who were also being drawn to reflect on such questions as "How do I combine professional excellence with whatever God is calling me to be as a spiritual person?" I shared their convictions that we cannot compromise our Christ-centered virtues in the interest of conforming to the expectations of a success-oriented, consumer-driven system.

Since the closing of the Institute of Formative Spirituality in 1994, it seems clearer to us than ever that divine guidance takes many unexpected turns. We can never predict with exactitude the outcome of fidelity. All we can say for sure is that God will stand with us, no matter the twists and turns in the road. He will send people like my grandmother and George Kelly to remind us of our direction and to guide us along a path chosen for us—if only we have eyes to see the way and ears to hear God's whispered invitation.

A ROADMAP FOR THE JOURNEY

In their search for clear directives and wise counsel, committed Christians find their most trustworthy guides in sacred Scripture and the writings of the spiritual masters. The message of a particular text may penetrate our souls with no more intensity than the "tiny whispering sound" that Elijah heard when he was seeking direction from the Lord (1 Kgs 19:12). Sometimes God's voice may stop us in our tracks as it did St. Paul on the road to Damascus (Acts 9:3-6).

Whether we perceive it as tiny or thunderous, the voice of grace invites us to surrender to God's call in our inmost being and to follow his lead. Then we shall find the peace and joy that only the Most High can infuse into our hearts.

Holy Scripture and the Christian classics give us a roadmap to divine counsel. In text after text, we learn of God's own response to our human concerns. Of particular interest to us in this regard is the Sermon on the Mount. In the eight beatitudes in Matthew's Gospel, we find eight basic steps to finding and following a God-guided life.[1] We have chosen to focus the main body of this book (chapters four through eleven) on these simple yet profound counsels for mature Christian living.[2]

Each of the remaining chapters also offers and elaborates on a specific practical directive to the God-guided life. While far from being "Ten Easy Steps" to certitude in following God's plan, these scripturally based, practical guidelines to divine guidance can be implemented by any sincere believer:

Step 1   *Dive deeper:* "Be still and know that I am God" (Ps 46:11).

Step 2   *Seek Jesus:* "Come to me, all of you who are weary and find life burdensome, and I will refresh you" (Mt 11:28).

Step 3   *Repent:* "Blessed are those who mourn; they shall be comforted" (Mt 5:4).

Step 4   *Hear the call to holiness and change your heart:* "Blessed are those who hunger and thirst for holiness; they shall have their fill" (Mt 5:6).

Step 5   *Give and receive forgiveness:* "Blessed are those who are persecuted for the sake of righteousness; the reign of God is theirs" (Mt 5:10).

Step 6 *Be compassionate:* "Blessed are the merciful; mercy shall be shown them" (Mt 5:7).

Step 7 *Be docile:* "Blessed are the meek; they shall inherit the land" (Mt 5:5).

Step 8 *Make peace:* "Blessed are the peacemakers; they shall be called children of God" (Mt 5:9).

Step 9 *Depend on God for everything:* "Blessed are the poor in spirit; the kingdom of heaven is theirs" (Mt 5:3).

Step 10 *Be a single-hearted lover of God:* "Blessed are the pure in heart; they shall see God" (Mt 5:8).

Step 11 *Listen and respond:* "Abba, Father! . . . Take this cup away from me. But let it be as you, not I, would have it" (Mk 14:36).

Step 12 *Be faithful to your call:* "I have fought the good fight, I have finished the race, I have kept the faith" (2 Tm 4:7).

In addition to Scripture, our book also features the writings of acknowledged spiritual masters whose works contribute a wealth of insight concerning divine guidance. Those who have successfully completed this journey can add important details to our roadmap. Much like experts at a local travel agency would alert us to lengthy detours and the best accommodations along the way, the spiritual masters help us anticipate the obstacles that retard our obedient response to the grace of divine guidance and cultivate the conditions that facilitate our free and joyful response.

We conclude each chapter with an original prayer-poem written by Fr. Adrian. May these words prompt your own prayerful meditation on the mysteries surrounding divine guidance.

OBEDIENCE TO GOD'S GUIDING WILL
Adrian van Kaam

Obedience to God's saving will,
Gift of the Spirit rendering still
The wildness of a restless heart.

Obedience, sweet and simple bard
Singing deep within a peace-filled song,
The ballad of surrendering what is wrong,
In the stubborn tedious repeat
Of disobedient deeds of secret pride.

Lift them into the cleansing light,
The crystal clarity of Christ's surrender,
Strong yet tender, to the Father's will.

Obedient love did daily fill
His simple life in Nazareth 'til
The Spirit led him step by step
To tread the dusty roads of Israel,
To share the boats that smell of fish,
That heave and plough with groaning bow
Through drenching waves and sweeping winds,
To bear with treacherous stints
Of Roman rulers, high priests, pharisees
Until they nailed him on a tree,
Bleeding to death obediently
For you and me.

CHAPTER TWO

Diving Deeper

Be still and know that I am God.
Psalm 46:11

The first practical guideline to divine guidance is: *Dive deeper.*

Two friends of ours enjoy snorkeling and scuba diving in the pristine waters of the Caribbean. We are the happy recipients of their adventure stories. They try to recapture for us landlubbers the experience of diving through the rough surface waters into the silent deeps where all is still and beautiful. The ocean reefs and shoals reveal an altogether different world where the divers are surrounded by undulating schools of tropical fish and swaying multicolored coral.

Diving deeper frees our two overworked friends from the distractions and demands of a doctor's life—at least for a little while. They leave their city and office troubles on the surface. Worry ceases in the stillness of the vast ocean. Tension flows out of them like air bubbles from their scuba gear. They experience not so much escaping reality as seeing more deeply into what really matters: the sacred mystery of life unfathomable by human logic.

For professionals used to practicing the active strength of doing, our friends enjoy the wondrous experience of waiting upon the natural rhythms of the sea. They say that scuba diving teaches them to be more patient. Just when it seems as if nothing is happening, the most amazing tropical fish will appear seemingly from nowhere, filling them with awe for the endless beauty and diversity of creation. One of them compared his experience to that of a "city slicker" plunged into life on a ranch, witnessing the miracle of a baby calf being born or watching eggs hatch in a hen house.

We all know how difficult it is for busy people to stand still, to listen to the surrounding silence, to wait for God to do the leading. Yet without this receptive strength, the patience to wait, and the courage of enduring the darkness of not knowing, we may miss the message God wants to convey.

One practical result of receptive strength may be a spiritual awakening. To do what God asks of us, we first have to perceive the direction in which we are to go. The way may not be clear. The waters in which we dive may be murky, but at least we can gain a general sense of our direction.

All of us have been graced on more than one occasion by such awakenings. These moments provide a necessary bridge between *receptive* strength and *active* strength.

Fortunately, we do not have to wait to travel to the Caribbean to watch such wonders unfold. Led by a guiding hand, we can dive below the surface-rumbles of routinized existence to ponder some of life's most crucial questions: *How can I become more attuned to these graced moments of spiritual awakening? If I catch a glimpse of divine guidance, will it change me in some lasting way? What am I to do after the Holy Spirit awakens me? How do I dive still deeper into the mystery of life without losing myself? How can I assess the past in relation to where God seems to be leading me? Where do I go from here? What am I to do now?*

THE RHYTHM OF WAITING AND ACTING

There are two ways in which to "dive deeper." The first is to wait upon the Lord for disclosures of faith. At times we wait without knowing where God is leading us or how we are to respond. At such times, and they are more frequent than not, we pray for the passive or receptive strength of enduring.

The second way of diving deeper is to take the risk of stepping out in faith once we receive what for all intents and purposes seems to be a divine directive. Now we must pray for the active or decisive strength of doing or behaving rightly in accordance with God's will. In both cases, we must plunge into the depths of our souls to find the place of calm and completeness where our Divine Guide dwells.

This means that we have to dive deeper into the invitations, challenges, and appeals the Holy Spirit sends us in the ordinary circumstances of our daily lives. As a rule of thumb, we usually do not have to go elsewhere to find God's will. If, as an exception, we are meant to go forth into an unknown land like Abraham, the directive will be clear. Normally, however, we can expect God to call us in the midst of our day-to-day world.

The discipline of waiting. Discovering our life direction is a demanding task. The answers to our deepest questions are not immediately clear. We must seek God continuously and with urgency. Yet the only response we may be able to give at times is that of listening with patience. The discipline of waiting makes its own demands on us. It says in effect that we are ready and willing to follow God's precepts for our lives, that we believe the Lord will not fail to respond to our heart's longing, if we seek him sincerely.

Our silent attentiveness may be broken by simple, childlike prayers for divine guidance. They signify our trust that God dwells with us in love. He is the Master Diver, guiding our plunge into the sea of spiritual awakening. As we move into the depths, we have as our lifeline the words of Holy Scripture. They assure us that we do not have to go into the sea of self-discovery alone. We have with us an excellent diving partner: the Holy Spirit.

In the time of waiting, we might echo the prayers of Psalm 119: "do not utterly forsake me" (vs 8); "with all my heart I seek you" (vs 10); "let me not stray from your commands" (vs 10); "be good to your servant" (vs 17); "make me understand the way of your precepts" (vs 27); "give me a docile heart" (vs 32); "give me discernment that I may observe your law" (vs 34); "disappoint me not in my hope" (vs 116); "steady my footsteps according to your promise" (vs 133); "your commands are my delight" (vs 143).

Scripture gives us the words we need to pursue the fruits of any spiritual awakening. In our search for divine guidance, we find that we have been sought by God. Thus we call out to God with all our hearts. We beseech his support while we are waiting for new light. We pray repeatedly: "O God, come to my assistance, O Lord, make haste to help me" (Ps 22:20).

These scriptural pleas suggest that we have to persevere during the time of waiting, even when the waters around us churn and it feels as if we are losing our way. Psalm 119 also stresses that prayer of the waiting heart must be continuous. One who wants divine guidance must be up "before dawn" (vs 147) and "greet the night watches" (vs 148). These words are not expressions of a spiritual weakling but pledges of a committed Christian intent on diving deeper into the mystery of divine guidance.

The image of night refers not only to the darkness that follows the day but to those times in which we do not know where God is leading us. The only thing we may be able to do during these hours of uncertainty is to ponder his promises, which we find in the Scriptures. We may not discern clearly the destination to which God is pointing, but the psalmist assures us that a divine hand is drawing us on: "Probe me, O God, and know my heart; try me, and know my thoughts; See if my way is crooked, and lead me in the way of old" (Ps 139:23-24).

The discipline of doing. There will come a time when we know in our hearts that the period of waiting is coming to an end and we have to make a decision. This movement into the active strength of doing is the fruit of a spiritual awakening. It follows the time of vigilant perseverance when we pray and allow God to take the lead.

The initiative here belongs to grace, but we must cooperate. In the beginning, when we make up our minds to follow where Christ is leading, especially if the decision entails a change of course, we may feel some lingering uncertainty—as if we were babies taking our first steps. All we know is that it is time to act in accordance with the grace we have been given.

At this point in our journey, we should neither expect full visibility of our final destination nor exclude the possibility of a fuller disclosure. Waiting with patient endurance is one thing; submitting to the risk of trial and error is another. To act as God seems to be asking is to trust that the Spirit will continue to lead us where we ought to go.

Perhaps an example will help to clarify this important principle of divine guidance. Chuck Colson, whose life took an unexpected turn after the Watergate scandal, experienced the balance between patient endurance (his own imprisonment) and active decisiveness (his commitment to begin what is now a worldwide prison ministry).[1]

While he was still in prison, prior to his acceptance of his new call, Colson asked a mentor where in the Bible he could find a particular text: "The Lord helps those who help themselves." The answer he received was that this text was not in Scripture because—and here was the lesson Colson had to learn—"the Lord helps those who *cannot* help themselves." In other words, only when Colson admitted that he could not do anything without the guidance and support of God was he ready to establish a new work in the church.

The turn of events Chuck Colson records in his books proves once again that our life call is a precious gift, known fully only by God. It is a mystery beyond the grasp of human minds. No matter how decisively and creatively we act in service of the Lord, our destiny is disclosed to us only over a lifetime. No one, least of all Chuck Colson, could have predicted the outcome of his disgrace.

God indeed writes straight with crooked lines. The full meaning of our call may be revealed only in the hereafter. Each graced disclosure we receive, whenever it comes, will still bear an aura of mystery. Each time we act as we believe God wills, we may have to endure a moment of doubt. Helpful in this regard is honest self-examination. We have to raise the question in our hearts: Are we acting in surrender to God's will or of our own volition?

From the beginning to the end of our lives, we will have to cope with a certain amount of ambiguity. The grace of action prompts us to ask in all honesty if we are trying to look for the right path or not. Despite the lack of certitude we feel, we may at times sense waves of peace and joy washing over us. This is one time-tested sign that we are likely to be in tune with God's will. Even when it feels as if we are floundering, in hindsight we can see, as Chuck Colson says in his story, that we are on the right path. God himself rewards our choice to be and to act as faithful disciples.

GRADUAL GLIMPSES OF GRACE

Each disclosure of our call gives us a clue to where we ought to be and to what we ought to do. Layer by layer we come closer to the core of our purpose in life. Each glimpse tells us how our here-and-now yes to God's will fits into the tapestry he is weaving. We merely stitch a thread, whereas God beholds the entire quilt in all its splendor.

Recall, for example, God's command to Abraham: "Go forth from the land of your kinsfolk and from your father's house to a land that I will show you" (Gn 12:1). All Abraham hears is a direct imperative, but what is he, an old man, to make of this?

While there was no doubt about what God expected of him, imagine the avalanche of questions that must have rushed from Abraham's mind into his heart. What would following this command entail? Dare he go? Wouldn't people think he was out of his mind? Or would they envy him for having been chosen? Why was it necessary for him to leave his familiar surroundings, the relatives and friends he held dear? What was the use of such a venture? Was it possible or only preposterous?

Abraham could have argued endlessly. Instead, our father in faith dove deeper into the mystery of God's will. He plunged through the whys, ifs, and wherefores to a profound level of obedient listening and decisive acting. He dismissed the poundings of his mind and followed the promptings of his heart. He trusted that God would show him the way to this unknown land and disclose something wonderful.

Detachment: the virtue that disposes us to walk in faith. The story of Abraham reveals a key condition for diving deeper into the mystery of divine guidance. This is detachment. We have to let go of our own agendas if we want to follow God's leading. Relinquishing control is not easy, no easier than it would be for an amateur diver to make the plunge from *terra firma* into the tempest of the ocean. Yet it has to be done if new beauty, serenity, and order are to be revealed.

Trust: the virtue that enables us to go beyond uncertainty. Abraham received an answer. He prayed for divine guidance, and God responded. At the same time there was no obligation on God's part to reveal all he intended about the covenant to Abraham, whose faith had to be tested. For every answer given by God, a host of new questions arises. Certitude in uncertainty is part of the adventure that awaits those who are willing to dive deeper. Either we trust in God's leading or we don't. The choice is ours to make.

Compassion: the virtue that sheds light on God's call. Abraham's story also demonstrates that God's compassion for us has to be mirrored in our compassion for others. We are all involved in the struggle to be detached, trustful, compassionate women and men of faith. Compassion alone can explain God's call to covenant love and its repetition throughout salvation history.

The story of Samuel provides an excellent example of this gentle yet persistent "hound of heaven" reminder of God's pursuit of a people. As a boy, Samuel lived with the prophet Eli. The Lord had to call the young lad three times before he answered with the words: "Speak for your servant is listening" (1 Sm 3:10). Samuel had to dive below the level of literal hearing to listen with a faith-filled heart.

God's triple call signifies that we can be called to a new level of detachment, trust, and compassion at any moment. The Father's love warms us like sunshine on a winter's day. We move in his presence like fish in the sea. All we have to do is to swim in these waters with childlike faith as Samuel did. We can then count on the fact that God will tell us where to go and what to do.

Once we recognize that "it is the Lord," our spiritual lives change for the better. The results are obvious. We do not try to confine God's will to a particular set of circumstances of our own choosing. We can let go of our need to find definite answers to every question posed by our greedy minds. We begin to trust that what God allows to happen to us in the present moment will turn out to be the best for us—for he can will nothing else than our good.

We also learn that what sufficed in the past may no longer be enough for today. If we try to repeat what worked previously, we may be frustrated. God may have a new mission in mind for us. Like Abraham, we have to "go forth" to the land where he leads us.

THE EPIPHANY OF THE PRESENT MOMENT

Jean Pierre de Caussade, the French spiritual master (1675-1751), refers to this single-minded search for divine guidance as living in the "sacrament of the present moment."[2] De Caussade says that God's will is not to be sought in the pains of the past or in the unknowns of the future. We need to hold the divine hand that guides us in our minute-to-minute life, in the here-and-now.

We have to seek what God is telling us in our real life situation. This is the highway to holiness. De Caussade tells us to wait upon the grace of the present moment and then to act on the basis of the awakenings and directives we receive.

The beneficial side of trials and tribulations may not be immediately obvious, but divine guidance never deserts us. Its full meaning may be hidden from us for a while, but we will understand more of God's direction if we listen with an open mind rather than with a predictable mentality. He says: "When we long for sanctity, speculation only drives it further from our grasp."[3]

To recognize God's will in the present moment, which in de Caussade's words is "what is most holy, best, and most divine for us,"[4] we must believe that the Lord himself is calling us, and that nothing he does or wills happens haphazardly. Though circumstances may unfold contrary to our expectations and understanding, God gives us the grace to cope with whatever occurs, to make the best of it. On the road to divine union, we are to profit from every joyful and painful event that comes our way. Idle speculation about "what might have been" blocks deeper listening.

The point de Caussade is trying to make is profoundly important. Rationalizing away God's word to us, without *affective* receptivity to the refreshing gift of his guidance, fills our minds with ideas but empties our hearts. We lose the rhythm of patient waiting and wise acting. We forget that the guiding will of God is not static but dynamic. It changes from one disclosure to the next. According to de Caussade, the will of God is "that duty [or disclosure], whatever it may be, that is now most sanctifying for the soul."[5]

Webster's *New World Dictionary* defines "epiphany" as an appearance or manifestation of a supernatural being, or a moment of sudden intuitive understanding, a flash of insight, or an experience that occasions such a moment. From Scripture and the words of a master guide like de Caussade, we can conclude that the *epiphany of the present moment* is thus a basic point of entrance to the mystery of divine guidance.[6] This privileged place of disclosure is the here-and-now. There is where we wait; there is where we act.

The epiphany of the present moment does not exclude learning from the past and planning for the future. All three expressions of time—what has been, what is, and what is to come—must be appraised if we are to dive more deeply into the mystery of divine guidance for our lives. God's leading is not a once-and-for-all event but an ongoing revelation that touches us where we live. Diving deeper into the present moment does not negate the unfolding of our life of faith as a whole. Any moment of waiting or any period of doing is but one manifestation of a magnificent story still being told.

Diving deeper can never be confined to one or the other "happening" as such; it is about being obedient *all* the days of our lives. No doubt there are times when the will of God lights up for us in a special and direct way, but such memorable moments cannot become the measure of our response. We are called to be true disciples in times of desolation as well as consolation.

Divine guidance is beyond what any temporal ecstasy can convey. It is like the rush of a mighty ocean streaming through every millisecond of our pilgrimage on earth. The more we see our numbered days with the eyes of faith, the less we are in danger of succumbing to false or confusing spiritualities. Without our realization, they may imprison and isolate us in the "now moment."

Even if "nothing" seems to be happening, humanly speaking, everything is, divinely speaking. In due time we will see, as in a tapestry, the threads that weave together the divinely guided moments of past, present, and future. This intricate weaving encompasses each and every disclosure of what our life call in Christ was, is, and will be.

Some of us are graced at times with a unique epiphany of divine presence. If we remember that our lives are a gradually unfolding tapestry, such a spiritual experience will not be exalted out of context. We will see it as episodic, as a prism reflecting past and future flashes of God's overall guidance in our own and others' lives.

The deeper we dive into the ocean of God's loving presence, the more we learn to rely on the graces prepared for us from the beginning. Grace is there to help us cope with cloudy days and stormy nights. There is no need to fear even in the darkest storm or the roughest sea.

HE'S GOT OUR WHOLE LIFE IN HIS HANDS

Why do the Christian classics insist on our staying in touch with all the disclosures of God's guidance? The reason is to prevent us from becoming depressed by the past, inordinately attached to the present, or sorely disappointed when our dreams for the future have to be put on hold.

Spiritual masters like Jean Pierre de Caussade recognize the immense, albeit superficial, appeal of pseudo-spiritualities that equate the present moment with "feeling good." Such an approach leaves no room for suffering or carrying the cross. Some sincere believers tend to equate prosperity with a sign of God's approval of their spiritual progress. We should see it instead as a passing pointer to the glory of Christ to be revealed to us partially here, and fully in the hereafter.

A life that neglects the search for divine guidance easily deteriorates into one long project of self-salvation. These people may shrug and say, "Who needs the burden of old traditions and ancient commandments?" Sadly, the spirituality of self-reliance can only lead to the dead-end streets of disappointment. Without the Scriptures to ground us in reality, one creates a fantasy world where everything has to go "my way"—not God's.

All of us can be tempted to let ourselves be steered only by isolated fragments of experience, mental snapshots of happy or consoling moments. Doing so makes it impossible for us to link our lives as a whole to the unfinished story of salvation history with all of its delights and its duties.

A master like de Caussade speaks, therefore, of the "duties" of the present moment. One duty is to see the present against the horizons of the past and the future—not as an isolated end in itself. The brightness of noonday does not make much sense apart from sunrise and sunset. De Caussade assumes that the present moment is but a passing epiphany of our life mission as a whole. This call comes to us from the God who made us and who has a unique destiny in mind for each one of us.

This larger call envelops every particular moment. It comprises our past, present, and future. All comes from God, is guided by God, and will return to God. Our faith enables us to hear and believe the words of love and hope expressed by the prophet Isaiah:

Yes, in joy you shall depart,
    in peace you shall be brought back;
Mountains and hills shall break out in song before you,
    and all the trees of the countryside
        shall clap their hands.
In place of the thornbush, the cypress shall grow,
    instead of nettles, the myrtle.
This shall be to the Lord's renown,
    an everlasting, imperishable sign.   Isaiah 55:12-13

In this spirit of trust in the providence of God, de Caussade writes, "each moment contains some sign of the will of God."[7] How different this is from saying that each moment belongs to *me*, to make of it what *I* want. According to this spiritual master, the present moment is excellent not because it is under our control but because it may contain a clue to the guiding will of God.

De Caussade contends that no variation of time, place, or circumstance can add anything to the infinite value of God's will. For this reason, he says, "The present moment is always overflowing with immeasurable riches, far more than you are able to hold."[8] We can behold these riches only if our faith is strong. "Your faith will measure it out to you: as you believe, so you will receive.... The more you love the more you will want [to listen to God's voice] and the more you will get [of divine guidance]."[9]

In no way does de Caussade fall into the present-day, popular heresy of "my experience" only. He would never think of the present moment as mine-to-do-with-it-what-I-want. This astute master says the opposite, namely, that "every moment the will of God is stretched out before us like a vast ocean."[10]

The desires of our hearts—stretching as they do over our entire past, present, and future—can never empty this vast ocean. The more we dive into it, the more our souls will grow in faith, hope, and love. This is God's promise, and it alone should ultimately guide our lives.

TIME TO REFLECT

The following set of guidelines will help you to dive more deeply into the riches of a God-guided life. Read them slowly and take them to heart. You may wish to make them a starting point for reflection in your spiritual journal. Try on your own to find passages in the Bible or in your favorite spiritual writers that bring each point home to your heart. Let these suggestions serve as sources of divine guidance for your own life.

1. See no moment as an end in itself to which you cling inordinately. Appreciate it instead as a passing but essential sign of God's loving guidance.

2. Realize that all variations of time, place, and circumstance make sense only if you are willing and ready to see the guiding hand of God in and behind whatever occurs.

3. Never draw a line of demarcation around the sacred mystery of divine guidance in a futile attempt to contain it in any one temporal moment. Instead, give God free rein over the whole of your life—the entirety of your past, present, and future.

4. Increase your faith by increasing your prayer. Faith is God's greatest gift to you. Believe that every moment is a pointer beyond itself to a lifetime of growth in fidelity to his unique guidance of your life in the context of humanity.

5. Learn to live in harmony with the situation in which divine providence has placed you. See it as the guise God assumes to reveal further reaches of grace, more profound invitations, challenges, and appeals: seedbeds for the cultivation of faith, hope, and love.

6. Ask in prayer for the gift of controlling what de Caussade calls the "despicable ego, the mortal enemy" of God's grace. Do not rely on your own human works—however great—that fall outside the will of God, for they cannot guarantee your satisfaction or salvation.

7. Try to develop an obedient disposition of heart. This will enable you to listen to the divine will regardless of how dry or elated you may feel. Know that what matters is not "feeling" much but trusting more in God.

8. Strive to grow in inner detachment, which will free you from self-centered ambitions. Use all your gifts in service of God's reign, regardless of what rewards you may or may not receive.

9. Rest assured that God will be at your side in all the pains and gains of life. Be convinced that not a single moment is under your control anyway. Try the best you can to be holy and leave the outcome to God.

10. Know that you will never be lost if you follow God's lead. Be as eager as the apostle Peter was to make your call firm. In this way, "entry into the eternal kingdom of our Lord and Savior Jesus Christ will be rightly provided for you" (2 Pt 1:11).

DIVE INTO THE SWEET EMBRACE
Adrian van Kaam

Apart from thee, my dearest love,
I am a lost and lonely dove
In a dark and dreary sky.

In the midst of empty time
Resounds the chime, the endless rhyme,
A sweet refrain of love:
Be still, be still, my lovely dove.

I know your days are rough,
The times are tough.
Let everything fall still,
Dive into my guiding will,
Chain your anger and despair,
Drain your pain, give up your ways,
Dive into the sweet embrace
Of my redeeming grace,
The silent boundless mystery,
The melody of empathy divine,
The groundless mine
Of gems of grace,
Outshining every trace
Of willful anxious pace.

Return renewed to the undulating life,
The surface noise of drive and strife.
Remember my melodious song
That lifted you beyond the throng
Of coarse distractions, frantic self-defeat.
Drowned in them, in faith repeat:
Before dawn I rise and cry for light,
My eyes watch through the dreary night

For guidance I believe is there
I cannot know yet how or where.

Make steadfast my heart of clay,
Straighten its crooked, feeble way.
Bestow on me a heart of gold,
Guide me in your way of old.

Every event is a luminous key,
A precious thread in the tapestry
Woven in time by an everlasting mystery.
How tiny is the thread you let me stitch
In the quilt of a humanity
Guided by you in its entirety.
A trifling word is my limping life
In a tale still being told
On which I have no hold.
Your answer to my cry
Evokes new questions. I wonder why:
How could the ocean of eternity
Be poured out in the thimble of a mind
That cannot even at will unwind
To dwell silently with the epiphany
Of your guiding light in history?
No longer alone,
I cry and cry, I don't know why.

Do not despair, spring's soft air
Is filled with sweet compassion
Calling to me repeatedly
To play my part since birth
In people's pilgrimage on earth.

Like a twinkling star in cloudy night,
Guide us nomads with love and light.

Enable us to bear the risks
Of going forth like Abraham
To unknown lands. Lead us, Lord,
Like the rush of a mighty waterfall
Crystal white and bright.
Send streams of guiding light
Through the milliseconds
Of an exploding cosmos.

Our numbered days, our wicked ways,
Unfold within its winding borders.
Yet we drift not orphaned and alone
Under the weighty dome, the relentless drone,
Of the star-studded universe
We call home.

Divine compassion is enfleshed
In your chosen One who makes the best
Of our wounded lives. He gives rest
To all who are complaining, pouting.
Without crying out or shouting,
He dwells in our homes, our neighborhoods,
He does not make his voice heard in our street.
Tenderly he holds the bruised and injured reed,
The smoldering wick he shall not quench.
Prisoners in the trench of a passing universe,
He guides them beyond the dungeon of space
   and time
In the splendor of the transcosmic shrine
That will be our everlasting home.

CHAPTER THREE

Standing Still While Still Moving

Come to me, all you who are weary and
find life burdensome, and I will refresh you.

Matthew 11:28

The second practical guideline to divine guidance is: *Seek
Jesus.*

When life becomes burdensome to us, when we feel weary,
when the load seems too much to carry, seek Jesus. In sad situations like losing a job, or being weighed down by the aches and
pains that come with aging, or feeling as if the fire of youthful faith
has flickered down to a few smoldering embers, seek Jesus.

When we need help, the Lord understands how we feel. He
tells us not to worry. He invites us to a new depth of intimacy by
simply saying, "Come to me." If we are thirsty, Jesus will give us a
drink. If we are hungry, he will ready a banquet table. We do not
have to wait for the assignment of a special counseling hour. All
we have to do is seek Jesus and listen to his word.

There is no charge for such sustenance. It is freely given, and it
ought to be as freely received. The prophet Isaiah declared the
same promise to the people of Israel:

All you who are thirsty, come to the water!
You who have no money, come, receive grain, and eat;
Come, without paying and without cost,
drink wine and milk!   Isaiah 55:1

Imagine yourself at the start of a busy day. You wash, dress, eat breakfast, plan your appointments. Amid the usual commotion, you feel welling up from within a sudden need for some contact with the Lord. What can you do? You know from Scripture that you can come to him without cost, without appointment. Jesus is there waiting for you. He wants to walk with you while you fulfill your daily tasks. You don't have to go it alone.

STILLNESS IN ACTION

When Christ is our center, we experience the paradox of at once standing still inwardly, in awe of our Beloved, and moving with him on our daily round of duties. Christ awaits our coming. He responds graciously to our need for guidance. He is available to us at all times. That is why we can be still while still moving.

To receive divine guidance, we must be willing to bring our whole lives before the Lord, to keep nothing hidden. In honesty and humility we must share with him whatever is on our minds and in our hearts. Prayer is our response to Jesus' invitation: "Come to me." Returning to the prophet Isaiah, we read in the next two verses:

Why spend your money for what is not bread;
    your wages for what fails to satisfy?
Heed me, and you shall eat well,
    you shall delight in rich fare.
Come to me heedfully,
    listen that you may have life.   Isaiah 55:2-3a

When we seek Jesus, we don't have to put on airs. We can be as open about our burdens as a child confessing his or her faults to an understanding parent. We may feel ashamed about the bad things we have done, but we have no doubt that we shall receive the refreshment of forgiveness. As we come to the Lord and listen, we are given life in abundance.

Christ gives us food for the journey on days when we feel weary as well as when energy abounds. All that matters is that we come to him trusting that he will "renew with [us] the everlasting covenant, the benefits assured to David" (Is 55:3). The bond between us and God will never be broken as long as we lay our burdens at the feet of Jesus.

Standing still in his presence, we are consoled. Refreshed at a table filled with good fare, we are renewed. We are ready to go where the Spirit leads us. This spiritual sustenance strengthens us and satisfies our deepest longings. We experience what it means to be still while still moving, to be listening with inner attention while attending outwardly to our work. We flow with the guiding wisdom of God while serving his reign on earth.

We learn to commingle a certain stillness and a sense of determination. The bumps and bangs of life are less likely to diminish our contentment and composure. We can stand in the presence of God without succumbing to the pressures of a busy world forgetful of what really counts. We can move with purpose and direction even if those around us seem to flounder haplessly. Whatever comes, we identify with a spiritual guide like Paul, who tells us boldly: "For our boast is this, the testimony of our conscience that we have conducted ourselves in the world, and especially toward you, with the simplicity and sincerity of God, not by human wisdom but by the grace of God" (2 Cor 1:12). Like Paul we want to be persons who claim God as our center and move with God as our guide.

Obstacles to obedience. What stands in the way of our being still while still moving in tune with the direction provided by our Divine Guide? The psalmist sheds light on the main problem we face: "But my people did not listen to my words; Israel did not obey me. So I gave them over to hardness of heart; they followed their own designs" (Ps 81:12-13).

So often we do not want to listen; we would rather walk according to our own self-interests. We seem to believe that human ingenuity in and of itself is sufficient, that self-help experts have the wisdom we need for living. The risk we take is that our emptiness may be only partially filled. The true guiding light for our journey comes from Scripture and tradition, not from popularized psychology, talk shows, or newspaper columns for the lovelorn.

Instead of seeking the Lord and following the lead of grace, we buy into the deceptive slogans of secular humanism. Disobedience blocks our receptivity to divine guidance. It did so in the Garden of Eden and continues to do so today. How can we follow the counsel of the Holy Spirit if we hear only the dissonant sounds of our own strident demands for self-improvement, to be all that we can be?

The voice of God is often muffled by the media. In a noisy world guided not by Scripture but by pragmatic goals and the promise of monetary reward, many people seek for happiness in the wrong places. What they find is not repletion and refreshment but depletion and discouragement. Is it not time to turn to the wisdom of a more substantial guide?

APPRECIATING THE ORDINARY

A contemporary spiritual master, Fr. Walter Ciszek (1904-1984), contends that God's guiding will is not hidden in a distant galaxy inaccessible to ordinary mortals. What we seek can be found in the atmosphere of our daily grind. *This* is our Nazareth, the place where Jesus dwells with us. He who became Emmanuel, which means God-with-us, walked dusty roads like the ones upon which we tread day in and day out. Christ awaits us in the pedestrian places where we live, in a world peopled by sinners and saints.

As Fr. Walter tells us, the situations in which we find ourselves are themselves carriers of the message God wants to convey. He had to learn this lesson the hard way. Being an American whose ancestors were from Eastern Europe, he thought he had realized his dream after ordination as a Jesuit in 1928, when he became a volunteer for the "Russian missions." To prepare for this work, he learned to say Mass in the Byzantine rite and was assigned to serve in Poland.

The priest's life changed dramatically in 1939, when the Red Army overran eastern Poland and Fr. Walter followed many Polish refugees into Russia. Disguised as a worker, he accompanied them in the hope of being able to minister to their spiritual needs. He writes in his book, *He Leadeth Me*, "I didn't fool the Soviet secret police. As soon as Germany invaded Russia in June 1941, I was picked up... and put into prison."[1]

Fr. Walter spent the next twenty-three years either in Soviet prisons or the slave labor camps of Siberia. He never thought he would see America again. When he returned to New York in 1963, he felt like Lazarus stepping out of the tomb.

This long and dreadful period of imprisonment and interrogation left an indelible imprint on this priest's soul. It forced him to find new meaning in the ordinary round of darkness and light, of death and life, that mark the human predicament and call for deep faith. Stripped of normal supports, Fr. Walter had to lean on God for guidance. He learned how to detect guiding lights in everyday practicalities such as food and water, in new friends, and even in harsh enemies. All were in some way emissaries of the sacred mystery, not haphazard circumstances.

Fr. Walter learned throughout his ordeal to rely on "a core of seemingly simple truths to guide me."[2] As he put it: "The plain and simple truth is that his will is what he actually wills to send us each day, in the way of circumstances, places, people, and problems. The trick is to learn to see that—not just in theory, or not just occasionally in a flash of insight granted by God's grace, but every day."[3]

While in prison, Fr. Walter learned to seek solutions for his problems—the pain of loneliness, the uncertainty of God's love, the pressure to make a false confession—not by escaping from them but by diving more deeply into them. He saw in the everyday events of his circumstances an arena in which to take up his cross and follow Jesus in appreciative abandonment. He learned from experience not to repeat his mistakes but to work for wise solutions, always mindful of Jesus' own dying and rising.

One escape hatch we often take is to run away from the blessing and burden of divine guidance to a fantasy world of perfect, self-made contentment. Our imagined protection would be short-lived. The first stone life cast our way would immediately shatter the glass bubble surrounding us. Real joy can be ours only when we build our house on the rock of reality.

Another false solution to the problems of life is to keep moving so fast that we either miss or avoid the call to slow down and appreciate the ordinary.[4] Still another kind of misguidance would be to expect some dramatic intervention on our behalf. We may expect disclosures from God only during extraordinary events. We wait for divine lights to flash on at special occasions, perhaps when we're on retreat, when we have to cope with the death of a loved one, or when we fall ill and feel out of control.

LOOKING FOR GOD IN ALL THE WRONG PLACES

Why are we so prone to looking beyond our ordinary, everyday circumstances for what we seek? Life's broken shells and debris are so common, so humdrum and routine, that we set out, in Fr. Walter's words, "to discover instead some other nobler 'will of God' in the abstract that better fits *our* notion of what his will should be."[5]

Nothing could be farther from the truth. As Fr. Walter suggests, God's guidance is present at every moment, always available to us for the asking. The Spirit speaks not only in our hearts but also in the prosaic events that make up any ordinary day. We do not stand on the shore looking out to sea; we are already immersed in an ocean of divine love and guidance.

What we must not do is engage in convoluted reasoning that arouses more disquiet. Instead we ought to grow in awe and appreciation for the hidden inspirations God sends our way every day. They are pointers to where the Lord is leading us. We have to become like a geographer adept at reading maps or like a captain able to steer a ship in stormy seas.

When we seek Jesus as spiritually mature people, we learn, on the one hand, a new art: to stand still and listen to all sides of the situation. We acquire, on the other hand, a new discipline: to do the best we can in accordance with the light we have been given.

However helpful humanistic techniques and counseling theories may be in addressing general human needs, the way of divine guidance takes a simpler approach. It aims primarily to help us grow in the imitation of Christ. For example, amid the demands of his public life, Jesus sought a quiet place to pray (Mk 6:31). So must we. When he could have grown discouraged, he accepted his mission with grace. Jesus walks by our side to enable us to do the same.

In his Epistle to the Colossians, St. Paul gives us the key to living the paradox of being still while still moving. "Put on then, as God's chosen ones, holy and beloved, heartfelt compassion, kindness, humility, gentleness, and patience, bearing with one another and forgiving one another... and over all these put on love, that is the bond of perfection" (Col 3:12-14). He adds: "And let the peace of Christ control your hearts, the peace into which you were also called in one body" (Col 3:15); and "whatever you do, in word or in deed, do everything in the name of the Lord Jesus" (Col 3:17).

In this way we live in the best of both worlds: We pay attention to God's guidance for our inner life in stillness; and we advance his reign on earth by taking the needs of others to heart and by doing good works.[6] God wants to escort us through the maze of daily demands, to show us how to stay on the right road, even when life moves at a hectic pace.

Recall the story of Simeon, a saintly man who spent his life waiting for the coming of the Lord. A single consolation helped him to survive the long days of abiding: the promise that he would not die before he had seen the Messiah. When Mary and Joseph took the Christ child to the temple, Simeon held the baby Jesus in his arms. He knew his waiting had come to an end and that a new chapter of the history of salvation was about to begin.

As you try to interweave the grace of contemplation with the flow of inspired action, take time to pray Simeon's words of thanksgiving as recorded in Luke 2:29-30: "Now, Master, you may let your servant go in peace, according to your word, for my eyes have seen your salvation, which you prepared in sight of all the peoples, a light for revelation to the Gentiles, and glory for your people Israel."

TIME TO REFLECT

In the light of what you have discovered about divine guidance thus far, ask yourself, "Do I sincerely seek Jesus in stillness and in motion, in contemplation and in action?" Then slowly read the following practical pointers. Apply what they say to your own situation. Keep a record of the dialogue that takes place between you and the Lord.

1. Grow daily in the conviction that God has a special purpose for your life. He cares for you and all people in a personal way. Do you trust that God loves you, watches over you, and provides for you personally?

2. Who you are and what you do is immensely meaningful in God's sight. Do you believe that your life and work have a dignity and a value beyond what you can fully grasp?

3. What can you do to turn obstacles into opportunities for formation? To change what must be changed? To abide peacefully with what is?

4. Imprint in your mind the words of Jesus, "I am the vine, you are the branches" (Jn 15:5). Deepen your awareness that you are involved in a person-to-person relationship with God which sustains you every second of your life on earth.

5. Ask the Father for whatever guiding light you need to maintain a life of faith, hope, and love. Recall the promise of Jesus: "Amen, amen, I say to you, whatever you ask the Father in my name he will give you" (Jn 16:23).

6. Ask forgiveness for any times you have missed the chance to see and follow the light of divine guidance in your life.

7. Recognize those times when you are too preoccupied with the ways of the world to pay attention to God's ways. Stop and ask him to help you to silence your heart so that you can be receptive to his word of truth.

8. Ask the Father, the Son, and the Holy Spirit to give you the strength to persevere, especially when you are on the verge of deviating from your unique yet communal life call.

9. Pray for wisdom and knowledge of the heart. Learn to appreciate the smallest epiphanies of God's presence in and among us.

10. Be at peace with yourself and others. Do the best you can to remain still while still moving.

INTIMATION OF GOD'S GUIDING DREAM
Adrian van Kaam

All day long we halt and move,
Captives in a groove
Of blind routine that wears us down.
Within, a voice is beckoning:
Stand still before my guiding will
Mellowing your frantic pace.
Be a hero of tedious daily tasks,
A hermit in your silent heart;
Don't hibernate or hide away
Dive back into your busy day,

Keep moving with a mind refreshed,
A heart of flesh.

Open your eyes to the surprise:
Love can overflow routine,
Intimation of God's guiding dream
For your unfolding here and now.
Put an end to empty sentiment;
Faith in me should be the guide
Worldwide for all who stride
Too fast, too anxiously, through the dense
Thickets of daily duties and demands.

Nestle like a resting bird
In my cosmic tree of guiding love.
Fly eagerly on high
To sing on windswept branches
The wondrous melody of wounded love
For struggling humanity.
Move as the busy bee
Returning to its hive,
Diving into flower after flower
To gather sweet nectar for the queen.
Look at the embers
Glowing in your tepid heart,
Remember the raging fire
Of your former love for me.
I abide with you still inwardly, I am
The center of your fleeting life,
The silent driver at your side.
I do not hide in distant galaxies,
I share your daily grind,
The distress of your worried mind.
My Spirit dwells in a swirl of events,

Most tedious and tame,
Yet turned into guiding stars,
Epiphanies of mystery.

Each small thing you daily do
Within the boundlessness of space and time
Holds a dignity and depth of meaning and effect
You can never fully grasp.
When it all becomes too much for you,
Grow serene enough to listen
To the gentle cadence of my voice
In your open, waiting heart.

Always interweave the grace of inner presence
With the ebb and flow of everyday events.
Fight the battle blest against the blight
Of injustice, famine, war, drug-infested streets,
The weeds of sin
On my defiled and desecrated globe.

Don't despair, rekindle hope
In my redemptive guiding light
Restoring dignity, transcendent pride
In crushed demeaned humanity
Endowed with transforming potency
By me, Redeemer of the earth.

CHAPTER FOUR

Repentance
Opens Our Hearts
to Hear God

Blessed are those who mourn; they
shall be comforted.   **Matthew 5:4**

The third practical guideline to being guided by God consists of one word: *Repent.*

That stark word usually strikes terror within our hearts. Even
without realizing it, we easily embrace the fallacy of trying to
absolve ourselves from guilt. We may try to relieve our feeling of
guilt by turning a blind eye to our sins. Or we may strive for "self-
salvation" through the practice of extraordinary penances, done
more to please ourselves than to express to God our sorrow for sin.

True inner repentance means mourning for all the ways in
which we have spurned his love. It is one of the most beautiful,
joy-filled graces we receive. It is the door that opens our hearts to
the lush garden of divine guidance.

While it is right to link mourning with something sad—such as
the death of a friend—this beatitude counts it also as a great blessing. How can this be? Why does mourning or repenting for our
sins bring us comfort and joy? Why is the blessing of contrition a

necessary prerequisite for being guided by God?

The answer can be found in our human condition. Made in the image and likeness of God (Gn 1:26), we are persons endowed with a spirit whose dignity and value in his eyes cannot be denied. At the same time, we are sinners in need of redemption. As persons dependent on God's love and forgiveness, we know that only God can rescue us from sin through faith in our Lord Christ Jesus (Rom 5:15-21). It is not we but Jesus who justifies us in the eyes of the Father. Ours must be a posture of penitence.

Peter spoke to this need when those who heard his message were convicted of their sin: "Now when they heard this, they were cut to the heart, and they asked Peter and the other apostles, 'What are we to do, my brothers?' Peter [said] to them, 'Repent and be baptized, every one of you, in the name of Jesus Christ for the forgiveness of your sins; and you will receive the gift of the Holy Spirit'" (Acts 2:37-38).

In order to sustain a contrite heart, many believers cherish the prayer of the Publican: "Lord Jesus Christ, Son of God, have mercy on me a sinner" (cf. Lk 18:13). Some Christians make it a practice to associate this prayer with every breath they take.

We find in Psalm 51 another inspiring prayer of repentance. Meditating on some of its passages will help you to appreciate more fully why mourning is a blessing. You can see in these words an itinerary of the repentant heart. This psalm begins with a plea for mercy rooted in the posture of mourning for one's offenses against God: "Have mercy on me, O God, in your goodness; in the greatness of your compassion wipe out my offense. Thoroughly wash me from my guilt and of my sin cleanse me" (Ps 51:3).

SEEKING THE BALANCE OF
FORGIVENESS AND GUIDANCE

Merely feeling the need for relief from our guilt and crying out for mercy are not enough. Taking the pangs of conscience to heart is only a first step. Regrettably, many believers stay on this level of guidance. They cannot quite embrace the second step suggested by the psalmist: that God really forgives and forgets our sinfulness if only we are sincerely repentant.

Have you ever felt that your sins are unforgivable? That you are not worthy of receiving divine guidance? That you long for a compassion you don't really expect to receive? Strong feelings of unworthiness often work against us. They can wrongly direct us to deny our very need for repentance. It is as if God holds out the balm of mercy we crave, yet we are too embarrassed to touch it.

Ignoring the call to true contrition, we may lose ourselves in escapist pursuits. We may develop elaborate excuses for our sinfulness. We may even decide that there is nothing in our behavior of serious concern.

Being so easygoing about sin is at one extreme of this pendulum. At the other extreme is the heresy of self-sought perfectionism. So profound is our despair over guilt that we feel as if we must first be perfect. Only then can we rightly ask the Lord for forgiveness. Rather than letting the Lord make our sinful souls "whiter than snow" (Ps 51:9), we choose the deceptive path of self-salvation. We act as if our works of penance will by themselves guarantee fidelity to divine guidance. Both extremes—escape in excuses or entrapment in self-accusation—belie true repentance.

Consider Buddy, a man so absorbed in his work, in sports, in one hobby after another, that he neglected the one thing necessary: to listen to God's call to be first of all a loving husband to his wife and a good father for his children. If his wife brought up any remarks about his behavior, he immediately bristled and the conversation ended there. He dealt with faint reminders of repentance by either stony silence or escape into excuses.

As time passed and Buddy continued to show no willingness to change, his wife became so overworked and lonely that she fell ill. Buddy couldn't handle the situation. He became depressed by his entrapment in an endless string of "what ifs" and "if onlys." He could not escape the despair of self-accusation. Yet Buddy did nothing to alter his ways for the better. He did not respond to the grace of repentance. He simply settled for feeling bad and regretting that he had allowed their family life to slip out of control.

To attain the right balance, we must both mourn for our sins and do something about them. When we ask for mercy and receive God's forgiveness, we shall find consolation in his compassion, as well as the courage to take responsibility for our sinfulness.

COUNTING SHEEP OR SURRENDERING THE FLOCK?

We must keep before our mind's eye not so much this or that offense as the overall sinfulness of our condition. A story best illustrates this principle. A young priest was hearing confessions in a small country town. Toward the end of the hour, a gruff farmer came into the confessional, blessed himself, and then said, "Go to hell: fifty times. Damn you: forty-five times. Bastard: thirty times."

No, this good man was not cursing the confessor. He had reduced sin to a quantifiable entity—so many units of this fault, so many of that offense. The priest granted the farmer absolution, but not before trying to help him see that these bad habits pointed to a narrow understanding of his connectedness to God. Was he truly repentant? Or would he return next month, thoughtlessly reciting the same list?

When the old farmer next returned to the confessional, he had taken to heart the priest's advice. "I confess telling my young helper to go to hell twenty-five times...."

A significant improvement! mused the priest.

"... but I went to him later and apologized for my bad temper," the farmer added hastily. "I said 'Damn you' to my lazy nephew probably once or twice a day, until just recently when I took time to sit and talk with him. It turns out that he wants to do a good job with the planting but feels he can never rise to my expectations. Best of all, I never once said 'Bastard' to my old horse! I brought him carrots and brushed his mane. You would have thought I was almighty God the way he nuzzled me!"

No, you are not God, thought the priest, *but certainly you are a man more guided by God*.

A few weeks after the second confession, the priest was invited to the farmer's house for lunch. Everyone around the table was in a jovial mood. The man's wife took the pastor aside and thanked him. "This place was like a funeral parlor. We spoke in whispers so as not to aggravate him. Many were the moments I rued the day we married. Now I see again his gracious side. It feels as if the Lord himself has entered our house."

The change in the farmer's personality had transformed the atmosphere in his home from one of gloom to gladness. After grace everyone ate a generous helping of beef stew and homemade bread. What might have been a mere feeding of hungry people filled with resentment turned into a festive occasion.

The anonymous author of the late fourteenth-century English classic *The Cloud of Unknowing* likewise advises us not to concentrate so much on minute details concerning what we have done or failed to do as on our being a "lump of sin."[1] Thus the psalmist mourns, "For I know my offense, my sin is always before me. Against you alone have I sinned; I have done such evil in your sight" (Ps 51:5-6).

A shift in emphasis, however slight, follows this acknowledgment as the sorrow of contrition gives way to the joy of consolation: "The bones you have crushed rejoice.... Restore my joy in your salvation; sustain in me a willing spirit" (Ps 51:10-14).

We see nothing in this text of sadness or discouragement. Repentance proves to be the seedbed of recuperation. It encourages us to place our problems against the horizon of the divine plan for our lives.

Repentant eyes see life in the proper perspective. We neither take ourselves too seriously (thinking that we are sinners unworthy of receiving redeeming grace), nor do we take God too lightly (presuming that since we are becoming perfect, we are not really in need of so much grace after all).

The balance we seek is portrayed many times over in sacred Scripture, such as this passage from the prophet Isaiah:

Yes, the Lord shall comfort Zion
  and have pity on all her ruins;
Her deserts he shall make like Eden,
  her wasteland like the garden of the Lord;
Joy and gladness shall be found in her
  thanksgiving and the sound of song.   Isaiah 51:3

Such gladness assures fidelity to God's guidance. It enables us to persevere. It renews in us "a steadfast spirit" (Ps 51:12). It sustains in us a willingness to flow with divine directives. It makes us more sensitive to the slightest deviation from the light God sends to guide our way.

Contrition of heart (repenting for having offended God) and humility (naming our sins and asking for forgiveness) gradually become second nature to us. We begin to walk in the truth of who we are, sinners in need of redemption, penitents aware that without the guidance of our divine companion, we would be lost. By the same token, we feel consoled by a generous outpouring of grace, and the conviction that our lives are going in the right direction.

CONTRITION AS THE START OF CONVERSION

In the first centuries of Christianity, the Church Fathers of the Christian East taught that *penthos* or penitence was the one disposition of the heart that could save us from the willfulness of sin and separation from God.[2] This disposition is the starting point for conversion or *metanoia*, which means at once a turning away from sin and a turning toward the guidance of God. It suggests that we are to place our entire being—body, mind, and spirit—under the gentle yet firm direction of the Holy Spirit.

Metanoia is a liberating response to divine grace. David, the shepherd-king, could follow the call of God only when he admitted, "I have sinned" (2 Sm 12:13). Peter could avoid the despair that claimed Judas' life only when he acknowledged his betrayal of the Lord and "went out and began to weep bitterly" (Lk 22:62). Though we may not be a ruler like David or a rock like Peter, we can always turn away from sin and turn toward the Lord.

The life of St. Augustine (354-430) offers a powerful example of contrition of heart leading to conversion.[3] Augustine had to make the choice of a lifetime. Would he follow God's will or his own impudent ways? The turning point came when he saw himself clearly as in a mirror: "Struck with terror at my sins and at the burden of my misery, I had been tormented at heart and had pondered flight into the desert. But you forbade me, and comforted me, saying: 'Therefore Christ died for all: that they who live may now live not to themselves but to him who died for them.'"[4]

Stunned by this truth, Augustine was able to pray: "Behold, Lord, I cast my cares upon you, so that I may live, and 'I will consider the wondrous things of your law.' You know my lack of wisdom and my infirmity; teach me, and heal me."[5]

Augustine learned an invaluable lesson in the light of God's guiding Word: "He, your only Son 'in whom are hid all the treasures of wisdom and knowledge,' has redeemed me by his blood. 'Let not the proud calumniate me, for I think upon my ransom, and I eat and drink, and share it with others, and as a pauper I desire to be filled from him amid those who eat and are filled, 'and they shall praise the Lord that seek him.'"[6]

Augustine shares in *The Confessions* his discovery that contrition of heart means more than mourning the loss of a friend or feeling sad when it seems as if one's mission, humanly speaking, is a failure. The call to repent is not about a feeling. It is an invitation to seek oneness with Christ, whose cross we must share if we want to receive the highest consolation: a truly converted heart.

This consolation comes to us through the dying and rising of Jesus. It enables us to resolve to do better every time we fail to respond to God's guidance. Sin is not a sign of failure only. In the light of divine forgiveness, it is a call to make a new start, as Augustine did.

The desert fathers wept tears of joy because in their contrition they focused less on punishment for sin and more on remembrance of the promise of God's mercy. Repentance reminds us that we are the undeserving recipients of graced redemption. It makes the illusion of self-reliance laughable. It tempers pride and arouses our compassion for others.

As the priest treated the old farmer with Christlike mercy, so we want to extend the same warm affection, gentle instruction, forgiveness, and care to our sisters and brothers. Thus from contrition and conversion there arises the gift of charity about which the apostle Paul speaks so eloquently: "When I was a child, I used to talk as a child, think as a child, reason as a child; when I became a man, I put aside childish things. At present we see indistinctly, as in a mirror, but then face to face. At present I know partially; then I shall know fully as I am fully known. So faith, hope, love remain, these three; but the greatest of these is love" (1 Cor 13:11-13).

TIME TO REFLECT

The following directives aim at a specific goal pertinent to divine guidance: to help you to become more receptive to the grace of repentance. Accept the blessing of mourning for your sins as a sign of consolation, as well as a confirmation that you are increasingly open to the inner promptings of the Holy Spirit.

1. To confirm the redemptive guidance of God leading you out of sin's entrapments, read the story of the prodigal son (Lk 15:11-32). Try to feel in your heart the welcome embrace of the Father.

2. Try for one full day to cast your concerns onto God and trust in his providential care. Meditate on the story of the lilies of the field and the birds of the air (Lk 12:22-31). Make a concerted effort to stop worrying.

3. Try to be who you most deeply are: a penitent forgiven by a patient Father. Then pick a good and bad day out of your week and let both serve as pointers to the mystery of divine mercy.

4. Examine candidly the times you feel downhearted or indifferent rather than repentant. Ask yourself if you are either presuming too much upon the mercy of God or feeling utterly unworthy of forgiveness.

5. Try for one day to neither exaggerate your troubles nor deny your faults. Sharpen your sense of humor. Don't take yourself too seriously. Remember the old saying that laughter is the best medicine.

6. Persevere in these practices of meditation while gently yet firmly engaging in self-examination before your Divine Guide. Catch yourself when you fall into self-centered defensiveness or inordinate doubt about God's direction.

7. Share with a trusted friend or small faith-group the reasons why you have come to depend on God in all things, no matter how small they seem.

8. Believe that every time you move toward contrition of heart, your Divine Guide rushes to meet you. Feel the dryness of your misery drawing down the refreshing rain of divine mercy.

9. Realize that whatever God allows in your life—whether consolation or desolation—he expects the same response: appreciative abandonment to the mystery of divine mercy, true contrition of heart, unshakable trust.[7]

10. Begin to experience the peace and joy no one can take from you (Jn 16:20-22). Like Mary, ponder God's promise in your heart: "Amen, amen, I say to you, you will weep and mourn, while the world rejoices; you will grieve, but your grief will become joy" (Jn 16:20).

REPENTANCE AND REFORMATION
Adrian van Kaam

Make my heart less earthbound, Lord,
My mind less drowned in small designs.
Let me run no longer after the seductive pipers
Of this small and narrow land
Of lust and arrogance.
Shake me loose from my rusty moorings
In worldly routines.
Shame me by the shallowness
Of a lost and empty life,
A sad succession of pursuits
Of earthly happiness.

Anxiously I hunted for fulfillment,
Evading me like a lark in flight.
When I thought I captured it,
The song had choked already
In its little throat.
Soon the graceful singer died.
I clutched only a bunch of feathers
In my grasping hand.

Grant the grace of sweet upheaval
To this dense and dreary life.
Let me meet you at the well of daily happenings
As once the woman did.
Create a new heart in me
That I may not return blindly
To all that used to be.

CHAPTER FIVE

Conversion of Heart Can Change the World

Blessed are those who hunger and thirst
for holiness; they shall have their fill.

Matthew 5:6

The fourth practical guideline to divine guidance hinges on a double directive: *Hear the call to holiness and change your heart.*

In the last chapter we saw that repentance marks the start of the conversion process. The self-justifying Pharisee in us gives way to the humble Publican. Now we can begin to confront whatever blocks our path to holiness. We can listen attentively to the Holy Spirit as we search our hearts: *What needs to change if I am to become like Christ? If I want to bring a message of wholeness into a broken world? If I want God's love to flow through me to those entrusted to my care?*

Only when we give ourselves—body, mind, heart, and soul—to God can he guide us in serving the good of others. Only when we hunger for holiness and thirst to do what is right can we enjoy what Jesus promises will be our fill of happiness and joy.

THE CALL TO HOLINESS

What is the call to holiness in our everyday lives? You may assume this question would be easier to answer if you were a monk or a nun living in a cloistered monastery. The rule of your community would define the expected behavior from hour to hour. A superior would assign your daily tasks. Your contemplative community would provide an environment that is sober, still, and simple. The steady rhythm of the day would free you from having to cope with the endless complications, unabated noises, and ever-changing demands of the modern world.

By following this rule of life, by obeying your superiors, by fixing your attention on the presence of the Holy Spirit in the midst of monastic life, you would have less difficulty hearing the daily call to holiness. How much more difficult it can be to hear the voice of divine guidance if you are immersed in the Babel of today's world. That still, small voice is often muffled by the agitation, ferment, and friction that seem to inundate daily life.

What, then, is the holiness to which God calls us in the world? It consists in seeking and following the will of God for our lives. This divine will has three aspects.

First, God knows and wills from all eternity our overall unique-communal life call. Before the universe began, eternal Love knew and willed the specific possibilities for goodness with which he would endow us. The Father guides our lives as a whole toward the image of holiness he lovingly chose and willed for us from the beginning. God is like a good gardener, who selects the seeds (our life call) that will blossom in the pristine sunlight of spring (our vocation, ministry, and profession).

Anything that happens to us during our lives is an opportunity, given or allowed by God, to make us a little more aware of what he has in mind for us. Each happening contains some expression of the mysterious meaning God intends for our lives as a whole. This divine meaning gradually unfolds between our birth and our transition to eternity after the short pilgrimage God planned for us on earth.

The second aspect of our call to holiness is our vocation or calling to a special state of life. Does God want you to be married or to stay single in the world, to be a priest or a religious? This general call then becomes more specific in different kinds of ministry. A religious vocation might be expressed in volunteer work or as a pastoral associate, while a career might involve being a millworker, firefighter, cab driver, teacher, business person, artist, nurse, physician, scholar, or writer.

In other words, this vocational, ministerial, and professional aspect of our call to holiness defines the fields within which we live out our overall life call in a unique and communal way. Vocations, of course, often change over the course of a lifetime. The married person may be widowed. The accountant may go to graduate school and become a professor of economics. The retired religious may enter a chaplaincy program.

The third facet of God's will for our lives is the guidance of God as hidden in the changing demands accompanying our specific vocational and professional fields. For example, a seamstress may be called to console one of her clients. A research librarian may have to handle the predicament of a homeless person seeking shelter. This third aspect of God's guidance adds divine inspirations to the first two. We are called to respond wisely and lovingly to the particular demands of people or situations in need of our attention, concern, and God-guided assistance.

Take the example of our friend Harry. When he was only twenty, it was already clear to him that his overall life call should make use of his concern for lonely people. He felt their need for warm encouragement and appreciation. God had given him a charisma or a predisposition of temperament and character to be an empathetic caregiver.

Later in life, Harry discovered that his vocation also included being a husband and father. His chosen career was that of a social studies teacher. Harry lived both his vocation and his profession in a way that was in tune with his overall life call to be a socially conscious person: he became a teacher in an inner city school.

The neighborhood in which he taught was continually threatened by gangs of violent youths. In responding to this turbulent situation as best he could, Harry came to see in the violence surrounding him yet another vocational disclosure of his divine life call. Now he is experiencing modest success as the director of an anti-violence peace movement in his own and neighboring schools.

Harry's story is an example of how all three aspects of God's guidance—the general, the vocational or professional, and the particular—come together in a harmonious way that makes a person's life personally and socially effective.

CONVERSION OF HEART IS AN ONGOING PROCESS

Obedient listening over the course of a lifetime is the source of ongoing conversion of heart. This continuing process is the hallmark of a true disciple of Christ. By the grace of God, we are wholeheartedly willing and ready to follow the path opened up for us by what we hear, to change our lives in the direction indicated by divine guidance. Each new turning to God entails a struggle with former dispositions that we have to give up if we are to follow new virtues inspired by the Holy Spirit.

Ongoing conversion of heart enhances our ability to hear each nuanced aspect of our call to holiness. Obedience means listening to God with a humble heart. Without the virtue of humility, we usually resist the grace of repentant awareness of our sinfulness. And unless we try to be true to who we are, we might never discover who we are called to be.

Without conversion, we forget that we need to keep saying yes to the threefold expression of God's will for our unique pursuit of holiness. We must continue to give our resistant, wayward heart to

God. Doing so enables us to walk in the abundant blessings his guidance spreads before us like a banquet table.

Conditions that foster ongoing conversion. The story of the Pharisee and the Publican illustrates the tug of war that goes on in our hearts as we move from self-centered love to other-centered love and service (Lk 18:9-14).

On the one hand, we encounter a complacent, self-righteous man, living in the illusion that if he only observes the letter of the law he can be saved—without the help of grace and without helping others. On the other hand, we meet a poor person aware of his own weakness, his inclination to sin, his unworthiness in the eyes of God. Hence, the Publican senses at every moment his need for salvation.

One man seeks the certitude of self-justification; the other hungers and thirsts for righteousness. It comes as no surprise to believers that God gives the Publican his fill, while the Pharisee goes away empty.

The lesson we learn from this story concerns the single-hearted commitment God desires of us. We must allow a passionate desire for divine guidance to overtake our other concerns. We must pray, as the Publican did, not only for the blessing of God on our frail efforts to serve others in a broken world but for a complete change of heart.

The longing for this depth of holiness assures ongoing conversion. Our daily yes to God helps us to relinquish the lie of self-sufficiency and to acknowledge our dependency on divine guidance every step of the way.

Psalm 17 echoes the plea of the Publican. The psalmist begs God to hearken to his prayer, to the outcry coming from lips without deceit (Ps 17:1). He cries, "Though you test my heart, searching it in the night, though you try me with fire, you shall find no malice in me" (Ps 17:3).

These words remind us that conversion of heart does not happen without a time of testing. We will be led in the night of faith into a profound confrontation with ourselves—with the best and the worst in us. We cannot hide from God nor turn away from our God-given destiny and life direction.

But how do we know what this is? Is our call the same as our vocation or our ministry? How do we bring our hearts into alignment with God's will for our lives? Such questions loom large in the night of faith. We pray fervently that God will find no malice in us as we try to be faithful to the unique call he intends for us. Even though we may have missed the mark, we want to overcome what is sinful in his sight. We want to make room in our hearts for God by letting go of fear. We want to trust that God will give us our fill of holiness.

The details of our call become clear over a lifetime. For now, we move from worry to wonder, trusting that we are at least approximating God's will in our vocational, ministerial, and professional life. The psalmist's words become our own as we turn from casual faith to a seriously committed life of love and service. With full hearts we can sing, "You, Lord, give light to my lamp; my God brightens the darkness about me" (Ps 18:29).

THE TWO FACES OF CONVERSION

Conversion of heart is at once an interior turning to God himself and an exterior turning to him in our neighbor. The converted heart hears the words of the Lord, who tells us that we are to love one another as he has loved us (1 Jn 3:23).

In other words, we cannot bury the treasures found in a heart conformed to Christ. We must share the fruits of inner conversion with others. They, too, hunger for what is right. They, too, are desperate for divine guidance. Their whole being is crying out for conversion. Injustice, discrimination, violence, and disrespect for human dignity bring people to the point of starvation. A spiritual famine gnaws at their hearts. They will never be satisfied with the empty "calories" of hedonism, consumerism, or moral relativism.

Thus the converted heart, one guided by God, moves from the

depth of a felt call to a vocation or ministry, career or profession, that aims in some way to transform the world in accordance with the will and grace of God.

The royal road to ongoing inner and outer conversion is love. The turns we must negotiate are unthinkable without charity. When others witness in us a growing capacity to care for them, they find it easier to acknowledge their own hunger and thirst for God and to care for others in turn. It is as if a vast throng of believing, hoping, and loving people begins to cross the desert of doubt and depletion to the promised land of renewal and repletion.

The converted heart asks: *Do I respond as Jesus would when someone comes to me with a broken heart? When I am empty, do I turn to God to seek my fill, or do I try to solve my own and the world's problems without his help?*

It is important to fan the flame of our own love for the Lord, while at the same time looking for creative ways to make others more aware of their hidden desire for divine guidance. As we express our concern in the context of religious or professional life, we can share our faith-stories with others and invite them to share theirs with us. The converted heart can empathize with others while leading them gently to a more trusting view.

Jesus reaches out to the woman at the well. The fourth chapter of John's Gospel recounts the story of the outcast Samaritan woman who came to the well outside of town.[1] Weary with walking, Jesus sat down and asked the woman for a drink. In the exchange that followed, something about him undeniably touched and changed her heart. So impressed was she by his knowledge of her life that she left her water jar by the well, went back to town, and said to the people: "Come see a man who told me everything I have done. Could he possibly be the Messiah?" (vs 29).

Inspired by her zeal, the people went to see this man for themselves. As John tells us: "Many of the Samaritans of that town began to believe in him because of the word of the woman who testified, 'He told me everything I have done'" (vs 39). Her neighbors were so impressed by what they heard that many more began to believe in Jesus. They said to the woman, "We no longer believe because of your word; for we have heard for ourselves, and we know that this is truly the Savior of the world" (vs 42).

This woman with a checkered past underwent a complete turnaround. This story teaches us that the guidance we receive from Jesus and lovingly pass on to others can be effective only to the degree that we allow the Lord to speak to them through us. Thus our hearts stay humble. We know that any good that happens is not of our doing; it is due to the power of grace working in us, using us as a channel to bring God's love to someone else. Conversion of heart thus becomes not only a unique but also a communal experience for the well-being of all those who travel the same path.

Jesus put it this way to the woman at the well: He will give his followers a spring of water that will keep welling up within them. They can then drink from that inner well every time they need conversion, every moment they wander astray from the eternal life granted to them by a loving God.

This ongoing conversion of heart purifies us as nothing else can. We gradually let go of the idle expectation that any source of power, pleasure, or possession alone can bring us lasting peace and joy, or quell the longing we feel for divine intimacy. Like the Samaritan woman, we, too, need to drink deeply of this "living water" (vs 10). Jesus tells the woman at the well that such water can never come from a cistern. This stream of love flows straight from the heart of the risen Savior.

The water of guidance Jesus gives us brings a special benefit: "Whoever drinks... will never thirst; the water I shall give will become... a spring of water welling up to eternal life" (vs 14). The Samaritan woman does not at first realize the magnitude of this gift. Jesus is not advertising a superior brand of water but an opening to eternal life. Her conversion is not confined to a one-time event; it will be ongoing for the rest of her life.

EVEN A SAINT NEEDS ONGOING CONVERSION

An example of inner and outer conversion can be found in the life of St. Thérèse of Lisieux (1873-1897), who chose the virtue of charity as the key to her call to holiness. She vowed to *be* love because "love comprised all vocations.... It embraced all times and places.... It was eternal."[2]

In her autobiography, Thérèse writes: "Just as a torrent, throwing itself with impetuosity into the ocean, drags after it everything it encounters in its passage, in the same way, O Jesus, the soul who plunges into the shoreless ocean of your love, draws with her all the treasures she possesses."[3]

Thérèse is aware that Jesus, not she, is the shoreless ocean of love. Her impetuous plunge expresses the utter freedom of a soul abandoned to God, but she still brings with her all her baggage, her limits and possibilities, her brokenness and her blessings. Thus she says: "Love attracts love, and, my Jesus, my love leaps towards yours; it would like to fill the abyss which attracts it, but alas! it is not even like a drop of dew lost in the ocean!... I cannot conceive a greater immensity of love than the one which it has pleased you to give me freely, without any merit on my part."[4]

The key to Thérèse's conversion of heart is her utter humility. She recognizes that she is being drawn into the wellspring of eternal love, not because of her merits but because God has loved her first (1 Jn 4:10). She perceives herself as merely a little fish in an ocean of love.

Like a sailor at sea drawn toward the lighthouse beacon, she is drawn toward intimacy with her divine guide. Hence she asks God: "What is it then to ask to be 'drawn' if not to be united in an intimate way to the object which captivates our heart?... This is my prayer. I ask Jesus to draw me into the flames of his love, to unite me so closely to him that he live and act in me."[5]

If we want to experience intimacy with the heart of Jesus, Thérèse's two-word prayer, "Draw me," must become our own. This intimacy is the finest fruit of a repentant, converted heart, a union between us and our guiding Lord. This union slowly grows and ripens until we can repeat the words of the apostle Paul, "I have been crucified with Christ; yet I live, no longer I, but Christ lives in me" (Gal 2:19-20).

The conversion of which St. Teresa speaks is first and foremost a work of love. Plunging into that ocean of love produces a continuous hunger and thirst for holiness. Nothing but God satisfies us.[6] Never would we settle for anything other than a life directed by and toward the Transcendent. We embrace the purpose of life as summed up by Jesus: to "seek first God's kingship over [us], his way of holiness, and all these things will be given [to us] besides" (Mt 6:33).

God alone can fulfill the deepest longings of our hearts. As Thérèse of Lisieux knew so well, our desire for intimacy with him is but a dim reflection of his longing to be intimate with us. How God wants to captivate our hearts, to draw us to himself in an exquisite life of union, to direct our whole being to his Sacred Heart! And he wants us, in turn, to live and act in the same charity and compassion we see exemplified in St. Thérèse.

Maturity in the spiritual life thus consists in doing the will of our Divine Guide with a disposition of childlike—not childish—surrender. St. Teresa of Avila, who was Thérèse's mentor, says that we remain strong "soldiers" waging war with the Evil One, but never forget on whom we depend. In Thérèse's unforgettable words, "in order that love be fully satisfied, it is necessary that it lower itself to nothingness and transform this nothingness into fire."[7]

Our hope rests on the promise that the Holy Spirit can enkindle our depleted hearts, reawaken our hunger for holiness, and remind us that in Christ we are called to be a "new creation" (Gal 6:15). Once we were lost because of sin; now we are found and justified because of the saving love of Jesus. Because of him our nothingness has been transformed into living fire.

TIME TO REFLECT

Now it is time for you to reflect on your own conversion of heart.[8] The following directives will help you to recognize some of the obstacles to conversion posed by sin. Despite occasional set-backs, persevere in your pursuit of holiness. The goal you seek—union with your Divine Guide—is worth every effort you make with the help of grace.

1. On the way to conversion of heart, try to focus less on your progress and more on your childlike trust in God's guidance. Avoid any form of self-centered piety that makes you more pre-occupied with what is happening in your isolated interior life than with God's call in your life as a whole.

2. Do not become lazy in the practice of spiritual disciplines such as formative reading that nourish your heart. Take time, even during the busiest day, for prayer and meditation so that your actions will be more Christ-centered. No matter how over-whelming your day may be, reading and meditating on even one sentence is better than none at all.

3. Never allow yourself to be absorbed by inordinate attachments to anything or anyone other than God, for nothing you possess in time can still your deeper hunger for intimacy with the Eternal.

4. Do not presume that you can walk the path to conversion of heart without God's help. Unless you immerse yourself in his endless ocean of love, you will feel lost and forsaken.

5. Be attentive to any sign of gloom, pessimism, chronic brood-ing, and excessive self-pity that dampens the fire of God's love in your heart. Discouragement, depletion, depreciation, depression, and discontent limit your trusting openness to divine guidance. *Important to remember*

6. Learn to downsize your problems by viewing them against the wide horizon of faith, hope, and love.

7. Work patiently from the center of your converted heart for social justice, peace, and mercy within the limits of who you are and what God is asking you to do in this world.

8. Deepen your disposition to seek ongoing conversion despite temporary setbacks and sins. Let sin beckon you to repentance and conversion of heart rather than drag you down to despair.

9. Be filled with gratitude for the graces you have received while never ceasing to think of ways to please God more. Consider also what he wants you to do in consonance with the dictates of the church.

10. Even if you have to suffer misunderstanding and persecution for the sake of Christ, be ready to accept the fire and light of a sacrificial life. Always try to do what is holy and pleasing in God's sight.

A HEART HUNGERING FOR HOLINESS
Adrian van Kaam

Lord, you read my heart,
You see the secrets of my life,
My lostness in lust and little things, not harmonized
In loving worship of you alone who can satisfy
The hunger of my heart.

O let me be within your loving spotless Son
A worshipper in spirit and in truth,
A candle burning brightly for the Lord.
Turn my days into a joyful celebration
Of the Mystery that is my origin and end.

Unite me with you, high priest of humanity,
Alpha and Omega, beginning and end,
Firstborn of all creatures.
For you have chosen me
Before the foundation of the world.

You are the longing in my soul, you are its filling.
Make me a messenger of the Mystery
Blending all creatures inwardly
Into a song of praise and adoration.

Let the radiance of your worship
Shine upon my daily doings.
Change the world before my inner eye
Into a revelation of your splendor,
Shining forth most brightly:
The destiny of all that is.

CHAPTER SIX

Forgiveness Melts the Barriers to Grace

Blessed are those persecuted for the sake of righteousness; the reign of God is theirs. **Matthew 5:10**

The fifth practical guideline for being guided by God is central to the Christian faith and formation tradition: *Give and receive forgiveness.*

Our faith journey inevitably involves some form of misunderstanding, persecution, hatred, and ridicule, especially when we take a stand against evil and injustice. We see this pattern in the life of Jesus, and he clearly warns us to expect the same treatment (Jn 15:18-20). Yet we are not to respond in kind. In this beatitude Jesus challenges us to view those who oppose us in a new way. He wants us to see persecution for the sake of righteousness as an opportunity to grow in likeness to him, so that the reign of God may be ours.

To the hostility that greeted his message of holiness, Jesus offered a startling reply: "Love your enemies, do good to those who hate you, bless those who curse you, pray for those who mistreat you. Stop judging and you will not be judged. Stop condemning and you will not be condemned. Forgive and you will be forgiven... " (Lk 6:27-28, 36-37).

Giving and receiving forgiveness is a central spiritual discipline, one which leads to Christian maturity. The words of Jesus suggest two more guidance questions for our consideration: *How can I forgive myself when I miss the mark or make a shamble of things in my own and others' lives? How can I forgive others as God forgives me?*

WHY CAN'T WE FORGIVE OURSELVES?

Let's begin with the thorny problem of self-forgiveness. Many people find it easier to forgive others than to forgive themselves. They can be so preoccupied with unresolved guilt about what they did or did not do in the past that they become paralyzed in the present. Without the relief that comes from experiencing God's forgiveness, they keep repeating to themselves, "If only I had done or not done this or that, I would not feel so terrible now."

John and Mary found themselves in that sort of predicament. The day John's mother died was the day he began to live in debilitating guilt. He grieved that he had not done more for her during her life. Why wasn't he kinder to her in her old age? He told us, "I know that I did not do for her what I should have done. I feel guilty about it. I failed her. Now she is no longer here to forgive me."

Rather than allowing grace to guide him to the blessed relief of sharing in Christ's forgiveness, John kept berating himself for his real or imagined neglect. His lack of faith and trust in divine forgiveness drew him away from God's offer of mercy. He became his own worst persecutor, wasting a lot of his time "kicking" himself for the "unforgivable" things he had done.

John's fixation on his "sinful" past made it impossible for him to become a more self-forgiving and compassionate person in the present. Ensnared in endless ruminations over unkind moments now beyond his control, he experienced guilt not as a pointer toward the future but as an imprisonment in the failures of the past.

Mary's story is similar. She, too, had a hard time forgiving herself, but for different reasons. She finally managed to extricate herself from a prolonged engagement to a man who could not make up his mind to marry her. Pride and social pressure had made her reluctant to give up the guy her friends told her was a "fantastic catch."

Mary had known intuitively, for longer than she cared to admit, that her relationship with Bill would not work, but she refused to listen to the inner voice of the Spirit whose wisdom she once trusted. The fear of loneliness had dimmed the light of divine guidance in her soul. Yet all the while Mary knew that something was wrong and that in some way she was responsible for it.

Early in their dating relationship, she had caught glimpses of the conflicts she could no longer deny. She didn't want to admit that her background and Bill's were as different as Jupiter and Mars, that their testy temperaments clashed at the slightest off-handed remark. Why hadn't she ended things then? Now Mary feels guilty about her lack of courage and her indecisiveness. She cannot forgive herself for being such a fool.

Instead of trying to make a new start, Mary can do nothing but bewail her unforgivable blindness and the waste of so many precious years. "If only I would have insisted on not seeing him anymore until we had set a wedding date, I would never have consented to our engagement. I cannot forgive myself for wasting all these years on him."

Both John and Mary feel guilty about costly mistakes they made in the past. They continue to torture themselves not for the sake of what is right but out of a mistaken notion of self-perfection. Neither of them can face their guilt—false as it is—as long as they imagine that what they committed or omitted is unforgivable. Instead of seeking God's guidance and the gentle touch of his forgiveness, both of them keep spinning around in a whirlpool of idle regret.

WHY MUST WE BECOME FORGIVING OF SELF AND OTHERS?

Healthy spiritual guilt—as distinct from the self-preoccupied reverberations of John and Mary—can help us to see ourselves realistically as sinners in need of forgiveness. Because we have been forgiven by God, we can forgive ourselves. Then it becomes possible to forgive others, even those who oppose us in varying degrees of intensity.

Wholesome guilt can result in new insights into who God wants us to be. The more time we lose in being upset about so-called unforgivable guilt, the longer it will take us to become forgiving people. Those who find it difficult to make peace with themselves—let alone others—miss the light coming to them from Scripture and the spiritual masters. The thrust of forgiveness is to move us from guilt despite past mistakes and disappointments to inner freedom.

Jesus tells us not only to love one another and to turn the other cheek (Mt 5:39) but also to forgive those who afflict us—not *seven* times but *"seventy seven* times" (Mt 18:22). Indeed, he describes a direct link between our forgiveness of others and God's forgiveness: "If you forgive others their transgressions, your heavenly Father will forgive you. But if you do not forgive others, neither will your Father forgive your transgressions" (Mt 6:14-15).

God has loved us from the beginning. He revealed his love to us by sending his only Son into the world that we might have life through him. Scripture says, "He loved us and sent his Son as expiation for our sins" (1 Jn 4:10). Forgiveness is thus a gift we receive. It is also a gift we bestow on ourselves and others when we or they are in need of this blessing.

We are not only to forgive our personal and shared faults—as difficult as this may be; we are also to forget or to let go of the hurt feelings that may result from any form of maltreatment. Forgiveness could be compared to the cleansing of a clogged drain. The dynamism of grace may grind to a halt unless we cleanse our hearts of the "sludge" of old hurts, paralyzing resentments, lingering bitterness, harsh rancor, and hidden anger.

God guides us in a special way in times of adversity or persecution—more so than we might like to admit. We heard the story of a woman who for twenty-six years had been unable to overcome her anger and "forgive God" for her husband's tragic death in a hunting accident. Her spiritual life had long ago reached a standstill.

Then this woman was given a prayer-word while at a retreat. It turned out to be the "trigger" she needed to reopen her heart to divine guidance. The word was "release." She had become a resentful person who, until then, had been unable to release the floodgates of grace-filled guidance. In a wash of tears she wondered what had taken her so long.

How many of us harbor resentment toward the people who have hurt us or betrayed our trust? Ask yourself some probing questions: *How often, instead of forgiving others, have I taken the route of revenge? What are my "weapons" of choice? If not "an eye for an eye and a tooth for a tooth" (Mt 5:38), have I used gossip for gossip, put-down for put-down, insult for insult? Do I really mean it when I pray, "and forgive us our trespasses, as we forgive those who trespass against us"?*

FORGIVENESS: A DEMANDING AND REDEEMING GIFT

This divine command to practice forgiveness is not easy, especially when someone closest to us—perhaps a member of our family or a long-time friend—becomes our adversary. As swiftly as a whiplash, resentment can replace forgiveness. If we let this poison fester in our hearts, we take the risk that the "reign of God" may not be ours.

Forgiveness of sin is, of course, an act of God toward us sinners. To forgive sins is his exclusive prerogative. By virtue of his divinity, Jesus assumed this right, though in doing so he risked the charge of blasphemy. "Who but God alone can forgive sins?" (Mk 2:7).

In his encounter with the paralytic, Jesus exercised this power, saying "Courage child, your sins are forgiven" (Mt 9:2). Even though the nearby scribes bristled at what they labeled blasphemous, Jesus spoke with authority. He knew they harbored evil thoughts against him, but his response was a direct claim to the divine prerogative: "Which is easier to say, 'Your sins are forgiven,' or to say, 'Rise and walk'? But that you may know that the Son of Man has authority on earth to forgive sins… " Then, to the paralytic, he said, "Rise, pick up your stretcher, and go home" (Mt 9:5-6).

Jesus passed this forgiving and healing power on to his church. Through the sacrament of reconciliation, the Eucharist, and prayer, the church continues to forgive sin as a divinely commissioned task. We are the beneficiaries of this great blessing.

Christ is ready to apply to each of us personally the "fore-give-ness" he gained by his sacrifice on the cross for our sake. "While we were yet sinners" Christ died for each one of us. Even before we confess our sins, he holds out to us the treasure of forgiveness. It is as if the grace guiding us beyond our sins has been waiting for us to respond.

The psalmist repeats what we already know from experience: that the Lord is surpassing in his kindness. "As a father has compassion on his children, so the Lord has compassion on the faithful" (Ps 103:13). If we open our hearts to our Divine Guide, he will grant us the grace to confess our sins and to amend our lives.

THE PRIVILEGE AND DUTY OF FORGIVENESS

The saints were often the first to recognize their need for forgiveness. In *The Way of Perfection*, we read a reflection of St. Teresa of Avila (1515-1582) on the part of the Lord's Prayer that calls us to forgiveness. Her meditation underscores the tremendous gift of this disposition of the God-guided heart. She says, "You see here why the saints were pleased with the wrongs and persecutions they suffered; they then had something to offer the Lord when they prayed to him. What will someone as poor as I do, who has had so little to pardon and so much to be pardoned for?"[1]

In the light of God's having forgiven us, St. Teresa calls her sisters to grow in "fortitude in this virtue of forgiving others even though [they] may not have fortitude in other virtues."[2] She finds it inconceivable that a person touched by divine mercy itself and realizing "the great deal God has pardoned" would then "fail to pardon [one's] offender immediately in complete ease, and with a readiness to remain on very good terms with him."[3]

We should see every occasion for accepting or bestowing forgiveness as a formation opportunity, or, in the words of St. Teresa as, "a favor granted by God."[4] To forgive is thus to give in the name of the Lord something of the love he has given to us. Indeed, for this excellent spiritual guide, the way of perfection is an intersection between two great highways: "giving [God] our will and forgiving others."[5]

Those who travel this road attain such a delightful relationship with God and others that St. Teresa says: "They don't want to remember even that there is a world or that they have enemies."[6] We taste a bit of heaven when we share with our sisters and brothers the bread of forgiveness. By comparison, how undernourishing—or even poisonous—are the crumbs of foolish feuding? What good does it do to strike back at our oppressors? How futile and damaging are our efforts to make fun of anyone!

Consider the little skirmishes around the dinner table about bothersome habits, picky neighbors, family decisions, eating habits, dress styles, or political opinions, to say nothing of out-and-out religious wars. Such battles are fought daily because people have not learned the lesson of forgiveness. Blind to the guidance offered by our forgiving Father in heaven, they persist in wounding one another physically and emotionally. Hearts harden like flint. Life loses its meaning. Many wallow in a misery of their own making.

Is it any wonder that we must pray daily for the gift of forgiveness as well as for the willingness to *accept*—even to *expect*—persecution? Such mistreatment is usually a sign that we are doing the work of the Lord. In the light of God's forgiveness, trust begins to replace suspicion. Patience softens our anger and irritation and quiets our inclination to quick reprisal. Forgiveness, in whatever form, is like warm oil poured on our own or others' wounds. It is sweet balm for scars of resentment.

But let us not be so foolish as to try letting go of resentment in our own strength. Especially in practicing forgiveness, we need to rely on the gracious mercy of our Divine Guide. We can rejoice with the psalmist that God will redeem his people from all their sins, "for with the Lord is kindness, with him is full redemption" (Ps 130:7).

In both the Hebrew Scriptures and the New Testament, the gift of forgiveness knows no bounds. The Lord does not ask us to do for others what he has not already done for us. When we forgive others, we are in a sense only flowing with the steady stream of forgiveness from on high.

FORGIVENESS AS A SPIRITUAL DISCIPLINE

From a merely human perspective, our initial reaction to persecution may range from irritation to rage. We may openly deride our enemies or secretly seek retaliation. We may lash out in anger or begin to build up a lava bed of hidden hostility, which may one day erupt like a blazing volcano.

Lashing out at anyone who causes us pain may at first make us "feel good," but the deeper result will be a dimming of our inner guiding light. In this case, proper feelings of guilt may surface, appropriate remorse that facilitates our becoming God-guided persons. It is never too late to listen to the gentle nudges of spiritual guilt, to seek forgiveness from God or others, or to offer an expression of sorrow over our own wrongdoing.

When the Spirit of Love becomes our guiding light, we are better able to accept the call to forgiveness as a blessing in disguise. In the benevolent climate of forgiving love, we tend to worry less about what other people may say or think of us. Instead of focusing on the words and acts of those who accuse or abuse us, we turn to Jesus for help. Instead of choosing the route of harsh retaliation or instant condemnation, we take time to pray.

Then we can calmly assess the best course of action. Perhaps our Divine Guide will ask us to leave a hostile setting, to shake the dust from our feet (Lk 9:5). Perhaps he will tell us to trust in the power of his grace to soften the hardest of hearts. Whatever happens, God's example of mercy will help us to contain our ire. Through his grace, we can avoid identifying with our aggressors by imitating their anger.

Freed from the paralyzing effects of aggravation and vindictiveness, we find new energy to go on with our lives and the work entrusted to us. No misunderstanding ought to halt our mission to serve the Lord with gladness. With hearts forgiven and forgiving, we can sing with the psalmist: "Merciful and gracious is the Lord, slow to anger and abounding in kindness. He will not always chide, nor does he keep his wrath forever. Not according to our sins does he deal with us, nor does he requite us according to our crimes" (Ps 103:8-10).

Drinking deeply from this fountain of forgiveness, we begin to view adversity not only as a problem to address but also as a challenge to change our own unforgiving approach to life. Such reformation is necessary if we hope to remain receptive to divine guidance. No wonder Jesus asked his disciples, "Why do you notice the splinter in your brother's eye, but do not perceive the wooden beam in your own?" (Lk 6:41).

FORGIVENESS IN IMITATION OF CHRIST

We will never become forgiving persons unless we are willing to share the cross of Christ. Pinned to this dreadful instrument of misery and torture, Jesus expressed not anger but empathy for the people who made him the brunt of their hostility. We, too, may be victims in our daily lives of the evils of racism or sexism. We may feel discriminated against or harassed in some way. We have a choice as to what action we may take: to forgive or not to forgive.

Persecution happens. Often there is little or nothing we can do to prevent it. What we *can* do is to use it as an occasion to provoke wise decisions about how to respond along with inner purification of heart. As Jesus said, the disciple is not above the Master (Lk 6:40).

Teresa of Avila often pondered the persecution inflicted upon the Son of God. She wrote,

What was his whole life if not a continual death, in which he always saw beforehand that most cruel death they were going to inflict on him? And this was the least of his sufferings; but how many offenses committed against his father and what a multitude of souls that were lost!

If one who possesses charity here on earth finds all this a great torment, what must have been the Lord's torment, with his boundless and immeasurable charity? And what a good reason he had to beseech the Father to free him finally from so many evils and trials and to bring him to rest forever in the Father's kingdom, since he was its true inheritor![7]

How terrible it would be if we were to deny ourselves the place reserved for us in the kingdom of God because we refused to show to others the love of forgiveness. St. Teresa expresses her conviction that the Lord profoundly reveres in us this divinely guided disposition. She reflects on the plea for forgiveness in the Lord's Prayer:

How the Lord must esteem this love we have for one another! Indeed, Jesus could have put other virtues first and said: forgive us, Lord, because we do a great deal of penance or because we pray much and fast or because we have left all for you and love you very much.

He didn't say forgive us because we would give up our lives for him, or, as I say, because of other possible things. But he said only, "forgive us because we forgive." Perhaps he said the prayer and offered it on our behalf because he knows we are so fond of this miserable honor [of ours] that to be forgiving is a virtue difficult for us to attain by ourselves but most pleasing to his Father.[8]

In this insightful text, the saint directs her attention to the root of our inability to forgive others as our Divine Guide directs us. It is our human pride that stands in the way of forgiveness more than anything else. The truth is that whatever we suffer has already been suffered by Jesus, more deeply than we could ever imagine.

Thus, guided by God, what have we to fear? Nothing we must endure—no pain, insult, or injury—can be as devastating as the suffering Christ took upon himself for our sake. Just as Calvary led to the joy of Easter morn, so our trials last but for a season. They come and go as God sees fit. If we respond to them courageously, our formation in Christ will deepen continually. The cross will be but a stepping stone on the road to resurrection and the coming reign of God.

We must imitate Christ's dying if we want to be worthy to rise with him and to enter his reign singing for joy. If we cannot endure and suffer the cross as Jesus did, of what good can we be in the kingdom? This seems to have been the thought of St. Paul when he wrote to the Corinthians: "Whomever you forgive anything, so do I. For indeed what I have forgiven, if I have forgiven anything, has been for you in the presence of Christ, so that we might not be taken advantage of by Satan, for we are not unaware of his purposes" (2 Cor 2:10-11).

In the light of Paul's experience, perhaps the order of the Lord's Prayer is not so strange. Immediately after we ask for forgiveness, we pray, "Deliver us from evil [from the Evil One]" (Mt 6:13). As St. Teresa told her sisters, all our fasting and praying count for nothing if we cannot swallow our pride, turn the other cheek, and forgive those who trespass against us—because God himself has cancelled our debt.

TIME TO REFLECT

Now is your opportunity to take to heart the wise counsel you have received from Scripture and the classics. The following ten directives challenge you to overcome the obstacles posed by lack of forgiveness. They offer you insight into how to persevere in the practice of this Christ-centered virtue. Won't you try to become a more forgiving person for your own and others' sake? Here is a way for you to do so, a way guided by God.

1. Guard against the feeling that anything you did, thought, or felt—no matter how unintended or deliberate—is unforgivable in God's eyes.

2. Remember that only trusting in God's forgiveness can relieve you from the feelings of guilt surrounding wrongdoing—provided you are sincere in your repentance and do not presume on God's mercy.

3. Be convinced that God does not want you to keep dwelling on the details of past faults once you have confessed them and been forgiven.

4. Do not wait in the wings, as it were, for great sufferings to come your way. Profit from the crosses that abound in the most ordinary circumstances of your everyday life, and through them receive and give the gift of divine forgiveness.

5. Acknowledge honestly the feelings of anger that arise when you are maltreated or misunderstood in some way, but try to accept such opposition and criticism without reacting defensively. Instead, respond appreciatively by making of these happenings invitations to form your heart in forgiveness.

6. Learn to appraise persecution as a disclosure of the life call God has had in mind for you from all eternity. Embrace it as a golden opportunity to bear the cross of Jesus, to grow in detachment, and to give witness to the reign of God's love on earth.

7. Rely on God to help you to forgive others when you feel unable to do so yourself. Never allow persecution to become a source of bitterness and vindictiveness.

8. Let your Divine Guide build a bridge in your life between the holiness you seek and the promised land of faith, hope, and

love to which you are being led. Know that what is happening to you has a definite purpose.

9. Trust that the meaning of persecution for your life's transformation will one day become clear.

10. When you feel discouraged, say with St. Paul: "We even boast of our afflictions, knowing that affliction produces endurance, and endurance, proven character, and proven character, hope, and hope does not disappoint, because the love of God has been poured out into our hearts through the Holy Spirit that has been given to us" (Rom 5:3-5).

GENTLE VISION OF FORGIVENESS
Adrian van Kaam

When I am the brunt of derision
Let me lift my anger in your light.
I need a wider vision.
My sight is narrow,
My feelings twisted.
I cannot see the deeper meaning
Of each event.

I hide in my shell
Like a frightened tortoise
Instead of placing my feelings
Against the horizon of the Eternal.
I pretend to be gentle
When I feel upset.
I live a lie
That twists and deforms my life.

However poor, it is this life you love.
Not perfect self-control,
Not phony sweetness,
Not fearful isolation
But an honest response
Of who I truly am.

Now I can hear your invitation
To lift these feelings in your light,
Mellowing my anxious strife
To reach perfection overnight.

I bring my guilt and self-affliction
Before your loving face.
No longer filled with rage,
I feel a wondrous cleansing,
Everything gaining its gentle place
In my vision of your forgiving ways.

CHAPTER SEVEN

Compassion: A God-Guided Gift

Blessed are the merciful; mercy shall be
shown to them.   **Matthew 5:7**

The sixth practical guideline to assure consonance with
Christ, our Divine Guide, is: *Be compassionate.*

Following the way of forgiveness prepares us to go one step further. Something more is asked of us by Jesus: "Go and learn the meaning of the words, 'I desire mercy, not sacrifice.' I did not come to call the righteous, but sinners" (Mt 9:13).

This "something more" is compassion. Once we grasp the depth of God's merciful love for us, he wants us to express that same compassion for others. This is the balm that softens the scars of sinfulness and suffering. As we show mercy to others, so they will extend the blessing to us in turn.

Ask yourself some revealing questions: *Do I sense the presence of the suffering Christ in others? Do I share their pain? Am I aware of their vulnerability? Do I know that the need for mercy is often hidden under a mask of self-sufficiency, coldness, and indifference?*

COMPASSION LIGHTENS THE
LODESTONE OF SUFFERING

No one could tell Gary anything. He was a tough guy, a hero on the football field, the idol of most of the girls in his class. Yet this was only a facade. Gary kept up a good front in public to hide the chaos at home. He had grown up with an abusive, alcoholic father. His mother, who had to support the family, was almost never home.

Much of what fell through the cracks landed on Gary's broad shoulders. He did most of the cooking and cleaning. He also took responsibility for his little sister. As her protector, he knew what he would do if his father ever tried to hurt her, and it wasn't pretty!

All this pain was pushed away when Gary left each morning for school. He donned the mask of a carefree fellow, a joker with a sack full of wisecracks, a regular guy dressed to kill. Then one fateful day the coach caught Gary alone in the locker room, shaking like a leaf even though the place felt like a sauna. He approached the boy with compassion, wrapped his quivering shoulders in a warm towel, and said gently, "Son, let's talk after you get dressed."

Gary tried to recover his composure before going to the coach's office, but to no avail. The moment he saw the warm look of sympathy, Gary broke down and sobbed uncontrollably. Letting the tears flow without reproach, the coach expressed his support by squeezing the boy's shoulders a few times. Then he said simply, "Son, tell me what's troubling you."

This embattled teenager hesitated for a second before removing his public mask. Then Gary opened the floodgates he had for so long held in check. The relief he felt in this man's compassionate presence changed his life. Even though his home situation wouldn't get better right away, at least Gary didn't have to bear the weight of that burden alone.

Despite appearances to the contrary, every person is vulnerable. Like Gary's coach, we can never be too compassionate. The lodestone of suffering we bear would drag each one of us to the bottom of the sea were we not kept afloat by God's compassion shown to us through others.

Listen to the nightly news, catch a few talk shows, read any weekly journal, go to the movies. It is as if there is no good news—only pain, famine, torture, death, violence, abuse, and every form of suffering under the sun.

Because we live in a fallen world, compassion must be a central disposition of our hearts. It is a sign that we are trying to live under the guidance of God. We read in the Letter of Jude: "Keep yourselves in the love of God and wait for the mercy of our Lord Jesus Christ that leads to life eternal. On those who waver, have mercy [or compassion]; save others by snatching them out of the fire; on others have mercy with fear, abhorring even the outer garment stained by the flesh" (Jude 1:21-23).

Our merciful God reminds us at every turn of the fragility of our existence. A plane crashes. A drive-by shooting occurs. An earthquake kills hundreds. Why were some spared and not others? How can fate be so fickle? There is no answer except compassion, no hope unless we keep the faith.

Picture the empathy of Jesus for those who cried out for mercy, and do the same. When people are treated unjustly, try to sense what they are feeling. When they are bent under the weight of worry, share their burden.

Picture the wounds of Jesus. Do you not weep bitter tears at his cruel treatment? Imagine the compassion his Father in heaven and his mother on earth must have felt when they watched the one they loved in such pain. Try to feel the same compassion when you see others in need.

THE NECESSITY OF COMPASSION

A world without compassion would never progress beyond the midnight hour, beyond the stage of merciless condemnation and competition. That is why we must drink deeply from the wellspring of divine mercy and pray with the psalmist: "But you, Lord, are a merciful and gracious God, slow to anger, most loving and true" (Ps 86:15).

Whether people live in slums or in wealthy neighborhoods, be they jobless or employed, all need the touch of Christ's compassion. Every human being at some moment cries out for mercy. Compassion makes us sense the pain of poor immigrants, the despair of homeless people, the loneliness of prisoners of war, the suffering of the unclothed and unsheltered—to say nothing of the silent rage of victims of discrimination in every walk of life. These little ones of God are mocked and marginalized as Jesus was.

In every person who suffers, we should try to see the suffering Christ. We should ask ourselves, *Lord, when did I see you hungry and feed you, or thirsty and give you drink? When did I see you a stranger and welcome you, or naked and clothe you? When did I see you ill or in prison, and visit you?* And the God of mercy will say to us in reply, "Amen, I say to you, whatever you did for one of these least brothers [or sisters] of mine, you did for me" (Mt 25:40).

God guides us to find the right balance between heartfelt compassion and wise acceptance of our limits. We can do a lot for others in line with our unique-communal life call, but we cannot do it all. We have to be careful that our compassion does not lead to overblown efforts to "play God." Neither should we nourish the deception that we can single-handedly right the ills all around us.

Each of us is blessed with a finite capacity to represent Christ's infinite compassion. Some of us are his hands, others his feet. Some bind wounds, others write books or pass laws in an effort to stop oppression before it starts. Each of us has a part to play in the symphony of divine compassion. None of us can possibly relieve and heal the vast array of suffering we find in our land, in our homes, in this sad and sorry world as we know it.

The important point in responding to God's guidance is to be faithful to our call. We may discern in any specific situation what

God *may* want us to do as part of our uniquely unfolding life plan. Rarely are we absolutely *certain* of that guidance. This uncertainty is in fact a great gift. It keeps us humble, flexible, and open to any change that may point us in another direction. Thus our lives gradually unfold in cooperation with the grace of divine guidance.

Abandonment to the mystery of God's will leads us, as darkness precedes dawn, to abandonment in the night of faith. There we wait in the uncertainty God uses to form us in patience and purgation. He wants us to appraise all aspects of our situation calmly and continuously, not impetuously or sporadically.

Our appraisal may in God's good time bring added insight into what he seems to will for us. Over the years we may discover, for example, that part of our overall life call is to be engaged in certain works of corporal or spiritual mercy. This means concretely that one person or group may address the physical needs of people through the exercise of care for the sick, prison visitations, outreach to the poor, and myriad other kinds of ministry.

Others may be inspired by the Holy Spirit to do spiritual direction, formative teaching, counseling, catechesis, and other kinds of educative or consoling works of mercy. Still others feel urged by the Divine Guide to relieve the ugliness and dissonance of life by their God-given artistic or musical skills. Thus each individual plays his or her own part in bringing the gift of compassion to a world in desperate need.

INSTRUMENTS OF COMPASSION

There are as many ways to be compassionate as there are needs that cry out for compassion. Different hands are necessary to mediate the limitless mercy of Jesus. When the guiding light of the Holy Spirit reveals to us over the course of a lifetime in what ways we can be his instruments, we have to respond. First comes the call or the invitation, then comes our responsibility to be faithful to the light we have been given.

Likewise, we have to be sensitive to when we are running on empty. We risk burning out if we do not take time for repletion. In prayer and silence, through conversation with like-minded Christians, and in quiet moments, we refill our reservoir. We remember that we are only channels of the river of divine compassion that flows from the sacred heart of Christ.

When we are uncertain of our direction, we need to turn to God with childlike confidence, asking him what we can do best to serve the needs of the community. How can we be effective ministers of his mercy? How can we serve others without becoming exhausted or betraying who we are called to be? Knowing realistically what we are competent to do, have we the courage to act decisively?

Our call may imply broadening our vision of ourselves as instruments of God's compassion; it may mean simply improving our expression of this virtue in the arena of action already revealed to us. To do what we can do best depends on our being prayerfully attentive to divine guidance.

Perhaps you are being asked to extend mercy to those overwhelmed by unspeakable misery in a third-world country. Perhaps what God wants of you is on a smaller scale: to share a cup of coffee with your neighbor. Compassion shown through showering gifts on those far off can be a lot easier than personally caring for those most near. Do you recognize this tendency in your own daily life?

Christ calls us to be instruments of compassion in our families and in the vocation or profession he meant for us from eternity. The compassion shown by fire fighters and cab drivers is as important to the Divine Guide as the healing powers of medical doctors and nurses. The understanding shown by bartenders is as necessary to the building of his kingdom as the sympathy of undertakers.

In the Parable of the Good Samaritan (Lk 10:29-37), Jesus poses a question to the lawyer who sought to justify himself: Which person—the priest, the Levite, or the passing Samaritan—helped the man who had been robbed and beaten? The answer is clear: It is "the one who treated him with mercy." Jesus then says to us, "Go and do likewise."

The spirit of mercy cannot be stored in its own separate compartment to be taken out and polished whenever the need arises. Mercy has to permeate our whole being. It has to affect all that we are and do. It is a spirit not meant to be kept to ourselves. Christ calls us to be generous in extending this balm to our fellow creatures and the whole world.

In their book, *Compassion: A Reflection on the Christian Life*, authors Donald McNeill, Douglas Morrison, and Henri Nouwen write: "In fellowship with Jesus Christ, we are called to be compassionate as our Father is compassionate. In and through him, it becomes possible to be effective witnesses to God's compassion and to be signs of hope in the midst of a despairing world."[1]

We cannot emphasize enough this guideline to divine guidance: In and through us, Christ wants to show mercy to everyone. Whether people share our faith tradition or adhere to other beliefs, all are precious in the sight of God (Ps 116:15). All bask in the sunlight of God's love and grace. How blessed are we who have heard and believed the good news: "Not because of any righteous deeds we had done but because of his mercy, he saved us through the bath [the baptism] of rebirth and renewal by the holy Spirit" (Ti 3:5).

IMITATING THE COMPASSION OF CHRIST

God-guided compassion extends itself to every human being in need. We may support charitable agencies that care for the sick or for victims of oppression. Efforts like these, however noble, are not enough. Making an impersonal contribution is not a bad way to show mercy, but God wants us to become more directly involved as well.

We should make a concerted effort to become more sensitive to the prompting of our Divine Guide to extend small acts of mercy in everyday situations and relationships. Is someone suffering and lonely in your family? Do you take time to listen to your own spouse or children when they most need your attentive presence?

What about the elderly citizen who lives across the street? Do you try to help her, too?

Compassion in response to the guidance of God can transform the world. St. Thérèse of Lisieux tells a story in her autobiography that underscored this truth. She describes how grace enabled her to overcome her reluctance to support an elderly nun, an invalid who was terribly demanding. She saw through the eyes of the compassionate Christ that her sacrificial life in the convent was of greater worth than a more carefree life in the world.

Choosing the way of divine mercy granted St. Thérèse an intimate revelation. She writes: "I cannot express in words what happened in my soul; what I know is that the Lord illumined it with rays of *truth* which so surpassed the dark brilliance of earthly feasts that I could not believe my happiness. Ah! I would not have exchanged the ten minutes employed in carrying out my humble office of charity to enjoy a thousand years of worldly feasts."[2]

Such concrete expressions of compassion help us to heal the disruptive, divisive forces that make our world such a cruel, discourteous place. This disposition is like a sweet waft of spring air. It binds the wounds we inflict on one another and on the beautiful earth on which we live. There is nothing we can think of—no relationship, no environment—that would not benefit from the soothing ointment of divine care and sympathy.

We must have the courage not to withhold compassion. God allows every human being and all of nature to share in the loving togetherness generated by Christ's compassion. He has designed each one of us from all eternity to be carriers of this compassion. Our ability to carry out that mission is a significant sign that we are being guided by God.

St. Peter sums up Christian conduct in these few words: "Finally, all of you, be of one mind, sympathetic, loving toward one another, compassionate, humble. Do not return evil for evil, or insult for insult; but on the contrary, a blessing, because to this you were called, that you might inherit a blessing" (1 Pt 3:8-9).

OBSTACLES THAT ERODE COMPASSION

What cramps the spirit of mercy more than anything else? The harshness we harbor in hearts not yet conformed to Christ. Nothing kills compassion more quickly than indifference or prejudice. These attitudes inevitably spill over into our behavior and make it impossible for us to follow the second half of the great commandment: "You shall love your neighbor as yourself" (Rom 13:9).

The more we ponder this theme, the more we realize that the three great enemies of compassion are harsh judgmentalism, competitive ploys to gain power over others, and divisive condescension. These three obstacles that seriously erode our ability to show compassion must be overcome with the help of grace.

Matthew 7:3 aptly describes judgmentalism as seeing the splinter in your brother's eye while not perceiving the "wooden beam" in your own. This obstructed vision paralyzes the natural flow of compassion. Prejudice builds invincible barriers of racism, sexism, ageism. One literally prejudges who is a sinner and who is righteous.

Christ condemns this behavior sharply, saying, "Woe to you scribes and Pharisees, you hypocrites! You pay tithes of mint and dill and cumin, and have neglected the weightier things of the law: judgment [justice] and mercy and fidelity. These you should have done without neglecting the others" (Mt 23:23).

Competition provides another serious obstacle. The competitive ways we behave toward one another make it difficult to live out the compassion of Christ. One-upmanship prevails in many relationships. This competitive sparring for primacy always subdues, if not destroys, compassion.

This obstacle persists in a society that prides itself on playing competitive games to gain power. We live in a world that preaches survival of the fittest. Business executives are promoted when they play "hardball." Who's the most charming? The best negotiator? The cleverest salesperson?

These are the people we are told to emulate. And yet Christ calls us to visit the sick, to weep with the sad, to walk with the powerless.

Our world points to successful appearances. The Lord asks us to look into a person's heart. Ask yourself: *Behind external failings, do I see the divine dignity of every man, woman, and child on earth? Do I celebrate God's underlying likeness that we share as members of the one family?*

Compassionate exchanges soften competitive put-downs. We experience the joy of laughing together, of working as members of a team, of celebrating one another's gifts, of fostering the dignity bestowed on us by our Divine Guide. No matter what worldly status we may have attained, we are all worthy of respect in his eyes. Can we not extend this same respect to one another?

The opposite of respect is divisive condescension. This third obstacle to compassion makes our success in society—if not our survival—dependent on lowering the worth of others. Such callous treatment is rooted in the assumption that to get ahead in this world, we must work *against* others rather than *with* them. We set up a "we-against-them" mentality that suppresses the less gifted, the weak, and the poor throughout the earth.

Judgmentalism, competition, and condescension keep us at a distance from those in need. These obstacles to compassion cripple our ability to hear the cry of the poor. They muffle the sound of the divine voice that guides us to the three conditions for showing mercy: *confirmation, cooperation,* and *communion* with one another in the Lord.

The cultivation of these opposite attitudes erects a trellis on which the vine of compassion can grow and flourish. Confirmation, cooperation, and communion inspire us to overcome, in any way we can, destructiveness, division, and disunion. Banished once and for all is the secret pleasure we used to feel when others failed. Lessened is our interest in the game of anxious comparison. Rightly do we feel ashamed when others are victimized by misplaced pity instead of uplifted by respectful compassion.

Our goal is not to make others over into our own image of what they should be, but to be instruments of Christ. We are called to enable others to follow the guiding light of the one who is the

Divine Origin of human compassion. And they in turn are called to enable us.

The mystery of God's mercy lifts us into trinitarian communion with the Father, the Son, and the Holy Spirit. Our faith dictates that we extend this gracious communion of love and compassion to the entire human family, as well as to the commonality we share with the rest of cosmos and creation.

The more we are guided by the spirit of the merciful Christ, the more we will strive to praise others when they succeed, to acknowledge our own and their limitations as mysterious gifts of providence, to exchange the words of forgiveness we all need to hear. Such mercy is proof positive that we share in the presence of the compassionate Christ, that his way of loving is becoming our own.

THE CHALLENGE OF COMPASSION

Why is it such a challenge to be compassionate? What fears prevent us from being as consonant with others as Christ was? What in us resists the flow of mercy received and mercy shown?

We may have convinced ourselves that compassion is a sign of weakness. People often say (usually when they least mean it), "Don't pity me." Or, "I can make it on my own. I don't need your help." Such statements betray a false understanding of strength—as if it excludes vulnerability and the human need for support.

To accept compassion is to take a risk. Our deepest fear is that we may lose control. We will have to forfeit our pretended identity of being the "Invulnerable One." We are afraid to give up the illusion of self-sufficiency. We resist admitting that we need others as much as they need us.

Do you recognize these tendencies in yourself?

To be compassionate means to give up a false autonomy that makes us feel superior to others. Just because we have more talent, status, material means, education, or honor than someone else does not give us priority in God's eyes. It is the humble who are exalted (Mt 23:12).

Compassion makes us aware of pain, that our flesh burns when it touches fire. It reminds us that our own needs and longings are not always fulfilled; that we are just as vulnerable as everyone to sickness, death, and misfortune; that, in short, we are more like our brothers and sisters than we would like to admit.

Probe your own attitudes and behavior. *What if people of my own class or family call me weird because I refuse to resist the pull of compassion? Because I want to help people no matter what class of society they represent? Do I dare to be different, as Jesus was? Will I be able to persevere in compassion if others put down my generosity as mere sentimentality?*

There are many choices to be made if you want to be merciful. It is so easy to become hard of heart rather than to be responsive to the guidance of God. Whatever happens on your faith journey, you must believe that the kindness of the Lord endures forever, that his mercy extends from age to age to those who love him (Ps 103:17).

A WIDE CHANNEL OF MERCY

Compassionate love can flow through us to others only if we cling to our commonality in Christ. Compassion teaches us that we are part of one another. In the striking words of the English poet John Donne, "No man is an island." Christ loves and saves us all. He wants us to be members of one family (Gal 3:26-28). This communion can happen only if we allow Jesus to teach us how to be compassionate as our heavenly Father is compassionate (Lk 6:36). It is our duty as Christians to rise above the cruelty that opposes such communion.

The fourteenth-century English mystic Julian of Norwich (1342-1423) saw singular and shared pain as an invitation to compassion. She took the risk of being a channel of divine mercy. This woman of God believed that the misery we experience—caused in great measure by sin—draws down upon us like rain in a desert the cooling waters of compassion. She writes: "As I see it, mercy is a sweet, gracious operation in love, mingled with plentiful pity, for mercy works, protecting us, and mercy works, turning everything to good for us.... Our failing is dreadful, our falling is shameful, and our dying is sorrowful. But yet in all this the sweet eye of pity is never turned away from us, and the operation of mercy does not cease."[3]

According to Julian, mercy belongs to the "motherhood of God," a sign of his tender love. Mercy protects, endures, vivifies, and heals. It raises, rewards, and endlessly exceeds what our human love and labor deserve. She writes that divine compassion distributes and displays "the vast plenty and generosity of God's royal dominion in his wonderful courtesy." And, she adds wisely, "When I saw all this I was forced to agree that the mercy of God and his forgiveness abate and dispel our wrath."[4]

TIME TO REFLECT

Now is the time to pause in your reading and to listen in your own heart to the call to compassion. Use the following suggestions to help you overcome hindrances that stand between you and your merciful Lord. Vow to foster the conditions that prompt you to become more Christlike in this regard.

1. Never separate in your own thought and comportment God's justice from his mercy.

2. Believe that receiving mercy and being merciful are two of the most healing forces in the world today.

3. Realize that God's compassion follows you all the days of your life. It is your greatest safeguard against disrespectful or offensive attitudes and acts. Recall the words of Julian of Norwich: "When by the operation of mercy and grace we are made meek and mild, then we are wholly safe."[5]

4. Grow in the insight that God's mercy and forgiveness are greater than the sins of selfishness and wrath. As Julian says, "In this mortal life mercy and forgiveness are the path which always leads us to grace."[6]

5. Avoid the hard-heartedness that renders you indifferent to human suffering. By the same token, avoid the emotionalism that so absorbs you in the anguish of others that you cannot help them in a sufficiently detached yet caring way.

6. Replace your overly dependent clinging to others with respect for their freedom. Try not to be a "pushy do-gooder," someone who shames others into being as "generous" as you are. Be suspicious when people praise you as a hero or heroine of charity instead of seeing you as an instrument used by Christ to advance his reign on earth.

7. Do not pretend to exude a compassion that does not truly emanate from your heart. Don't humiliate the poor. Help them to restore their sense of inner worth and dignity. Let compassion be uplifting, never condescending.

8. Share time and space to assist others in need. Teach them how to be faithful to their own unique-communal life call, no matter how small and simple it may be in the eyes of the more learned, well-to-do, and powerful of this world. Let your compassion be empowering, not debilitating.

9. Practice non-judgmental listening. Resist the tendency to make quick assessments of others. Establish and maintain wise, respectful boundaries. Be sure that compassion does not deteriorate into crippling relationships of dominance or submission.

10. Stay humble. Do not lose sight of your own vulnerability. Continue to be and act, in the words of Henri Nouwen, as a "wounded healer." Do not deceive yourself into thinking that you are superhuman or superior to those you are trying to help.

WITNESS FOR YOUR MERCY
Adrian van Kaam

Thank you for the dawning of your Spirit
Who lets us witness to your light,
Heralding your journey through humanity,
Proclaiming the mystery of mercy
That transfigures earth invisibly
At its hidden core.

Let us not betray your compassion
By coercion of an anxious soul.
The witness of mercy should be gracious and mild
Leaving space to surrender or resist
Your invitation to a luminous form of risen life.

Let our dwelling on this earth
Refract the soft light of your mercy
Like a stained glass window filters
The radiance of the sun into countless colors.
Make us light up uniquely the corner of the universe
Where we are placed in time and space
Like candles in a dark and empty hall,
Laying down our lives little by little
In compassion for all who pass our way in history.

Let our love be strong and honest,
Never a refuge from reality and suffering,
Not sentimental but right and fair,
So that not we but you may rise in the heart
Of multitudes in search of
Mercy for their lives.

CHAPTER EIGHT

Meekness Keeps Our Hearts Teachable

Blessed are the meek; they shall inherit the land.   **Matthew 5:5**

The seventh guideline to divine guidance reminds us of another basic condition for receiving direction: *Be docile.*

We all struggle with complete submission of our minds and hearts to the guiding will of God. Appreciative abandonment to the mystery does not mean giving up our responsibility or sense of duty. It simply means cultivating a docile disposition that keeps our hearts teachable. Docility makes listening and learning possible.

We see this same principle at work in secular vocations. For example, an apprentice carpenter conscientiously defers to the skills of a master builder in order to learn a new trade. A culinary student enthusiastically emulates the techniques of a master chef. Similarly, believers on the way to Christlike commitment willingly seek and readily follow their Divine Guide.

Ask yourself some searching questions about your own disposition of mind and heart: *What is my style of discipleship? Am I beginning to see in myself a gradual shift from gruffness to graciousness, from dominance to docility, from mastery to meekness? Do I truly want to grow in the gentle-heartedness of Jesus? Whose guiding light do I want and choose to follow? My own or the Master's?*

MOSES: A GOD-MOLDED PERSON

The word "meekness" usually brings to mind images of slavish servility, wishy-washy indecisiveness, or outright cowardice. Nothing could be farther from the truth. Jesus certainly displayed none of these characteristics, yet he specifically described himself as "meek and humble of heart" (Mt 11:29).

According to the Scriptures, meekness literally means "God-molded." And this beatitude assures us that only the meek can enter the land of likeness to the Most High. This is the land Jesus offers to us as our inheritance. Enjoyment of this promise is the fruit of intimate friendship with the triune God, with the Mystery that makes us be. In the words of the prophet Isaiah: "The lowly will ever find joy in the Lord, and the poor rejoice in the Holy One of Israel" (Is 29:19).

The Hebrew Scriptures depict Moses as a meek man. Because he was willing to be tamed by God, he could become a messenger of the Holy One to the people of Israel. "For his trustworthiness and meekness God selected him from all mankind" (Sir 45:4). Moses was also docile, willing to be taught or guided by God. He had to learn to exercise flexible yet vigilant self-control while not trying to control God's ways of relating to him.

Earlier descriptions of Moses suggest a strong stubborn streak, yet his whole being became so meek and docile that his countenance radiated the light of the Lord. The Book of Exodus tells us that "Moses stayed with the Lord for forty days and forty nights, without eating any food or drinking any water, and he wrote on the tablets the words of the covenant, the ten commandments" (Ex 34:28). When he descended from the mountain, something extraordinary occurred: "As Moses came down from Mount Sinai with the two tablets of the commandments in his hands, he did not know that the skin of his face had become radiant while he conversed with the Lord" (Ex 34:29).

This visible glow had an immediate effect on the people who beheld him: "When Aaron, then, and the other Israelites saw Moses and noticed how radiant the skin of his face had become, they were afraid to come near him. Only after Moses called to them did Aaron and all the rulers of the community come back to him" (Ex 34:30-31).

One face of the virtue of meekness is the *docility* that enables us to receive and to radiate the inner life and excellence of our Divine Guide. But this does not tell the whole story. The other face of docility is *durability* and *determination* in carrying out what we receive.

Moses demonstrated this determination when he came down from the mountain and discovered that the people had disobeyed every rule of discipleship and erected an idol, a golden calf. His strong commitment to be God's messenger broke through the submissive side of his meekness (Ex 32). Moses was furious that this fearful people had rebelled. In choosing idolatry, Israel had rejected the leadership of Yahweh through his chosen servant. Meek though he was, Moses immediately smashed the idol to bits. He defended God's honor and reclaimed for the chosen people the unarguable truth that their only guide was Yahweh.

The radiance on Moses' countenance was not just a passing phenomenon. He subsequently had to veil his face after each visit to the tabernacle where he conversed with the Lord. These repeated instances of divine radiance offer stunning testimony to the inner light that shines in a God-molded person. But the picture would be incomplete if it did not include the power and strength in Moses' arm as he trashed the false idol. Both meekness and strength tell us something about the power God grants to those destined to be his messengers.

MEEKNESS AND STRENGTH IN MOTHER AND SON

We see the same combination of docility and determination in Mary and in Jesus. To "live in a manner worthy of the call [we] have received" (Eph 4:1), we need to become less self-directed and more God-guided. We need to imitate the lowliness of Mary for whom the Almighty did great things (Lk 1:49).

Because Mary was meek, God could become embodied in her womb. Without her cooperation—without her free assent to the glad tidings she received—the evangelist John could not have written: "And the Word became flesh and made his dwelling among us" (Jn 1:14). And without her durability and determination, she would not have been able to walk the difficult road ahead.

We cannot imitate either the docility or the determination of Mary if we think that life means only entering a land of our own making. This would be a stark contrast to the land that Jesus promises shall be ours if we remain meek and molded by God. Ask yourself in humility and honesty, *Am I content to wait upon an overshadowing of the Holy Spirit to guide me?*

The obstacle we face arises from a common human tendency: forcing life to conform to *our* pace instead of the pace set for us by grace. How many times do we treat others harshly because they fail to measure up to our expectations? And aren't we usually hardest on ourselves, impatient with our slow progress in overcoming our weaknesses? Ask yourself: *Am I as gentle with myself as Jesus is with me?*

We need to respond to questions raised by our Divine Guide in a spirit of loving docility. Are we receptive to God's answers when he tells us what in us has to change? Or do we negotiate or temporize or pursue what strikes us as a better game plan—all in the honest pursuit of holiness, of course?

The more we practice meekness, the more our likeness to the Lord deepens. Even strangers may become aware that something seems different about us. Picture how Mary must have looked when she accepted the angel's message, when she carried the child in her womb, when she gave birth. What a glow must have surrounded this woman, who was at once submissive and strong. Because of her lowliness, God raised her to high places (Lk 1:52).

Often we are inclined to confuse meekness with shy, retiring comportment. Did Mary run from the angel Gabriel? Did Jesus hide from his accusers? Yet both were meeker than we will ever be. It was through their seeming powerlessness that God released the mighty power to redeem the world.

Belief in Christ marks us with the seal of meekness. Jesus calls us to become like little children, whom he proclaims as first in the kingdom of heaven (Mt 18:1-4). Those who follow him as disciples are called to radiate this same kind of simplicity, guilelessness, and trust.

As we enter the land of likeness that is our inheritance from the beginning of time, we meet the Lord. We encounter Mary. We keep company with the saints. We walk with the lowly and humble who found favor with God (Sir 3:18). Nothing that smacks of arrogance ought to stand between God's guidance and our obedience.

Modeling our lives on the Lord, on Mary who is the first disciple, and on the "cloud of witnesses" of whom Paul speaks (Heb 12:1) helps us to grow in the virtue of meekness. For Christians, lowliness or humility is the basic disposition that leads us out of the bondage of self-centeredness and into the liberation of the children of God (Rom 8:21).

THE RIGHTEOUS ANGER OF JESUS

God made our human nature in such a way that we become angry, as Jesus did, in the face of a terribly unjust situation. What is not right should be challenged and, if possible, changed. But we must be careful to do so without opening the door of our hearts to maintaining dominance by anger alone. We often have trouble balancing the meekness of the servant who washes feet (Jn 13:1-11) with the boldness of the Christian who strives to bring justice to an unjust world out of love for God.

Jesus demonstrated righteous yet loving anger against the money changers who were desecrating the house of his Father. He hated their sin, yet he still loved them as misguided people in need of redemption. They had to be shown in unmistakable terms how off the track they were, but Jesus did not close his heart to them. On the contrary, he desired their salvation so much that he was willing to risk his own safety as well as his reputation for their sake.

In other words, Jesus was angry about what the money changers did. They defaced his Father's house. But he did not nurse a grudge or cultivate lasting anger. Jesus forcefully expressed his outrage while shutting the door of his heart to the tidal wave of bitter resentment for sinners, anger that would have excluded them from his love. In fact, he loved sinners to the point of being willing to die on the cross for them.

At times we may assume that we can feel and do as Jesus, imagining that our anger is as righteous and loving as his. Hence we may not try to control it. This would be wrong. Knowing our weak nature, we should not presume that our anger is pure. More likely it is mixed with pride, lust for power, envy, and resentment born from past abuses we may have suffered.

Even what looks like righteous anger may be mixed unwittingly with ulterior motives. You need only probe a little more deeply to uncover the impurities: *How much do I want to appear tough? Does my expression of anger show too much pride and self-centeredness? Is my rage due to a lifetime of stifled resentment that I never worked through by submitting it to the light and love of the Holy Spirit? Does my rage leave reminders of pain in the people around me? In the worst case, does my anger become abusive in deeds or words? Is there anything in it of the rage of the angry mob that crucified the Lord? Does the indignation of the crowd fuel my own fury?*

No matter how far we have traveled on our spiritual journey, our inner life is not as consonant with the guiding Spirit as that of Jesus. Having intimately communed with his Father, the Son was sure that he should act as he did. It is far more difficult for us to have that certitude. Before we know it, we have opened our hearts to destructive expressions of anger rather than those that are righteous and loving. How easily anger can tear apart relationships. It can wash over us like a fire storm when we least expect it.

THE ENIGMA OF MEEKNESS

The virtue of meekness is enigmatic. People bristle when they hear words that clash with their cultural values. Their minds automatically register some argument whenever they hear words like gentleness (*Assertiveness is better,* they assure themselves.), lowliness (*People will think I'm weak!*), meekness (*They'll walk all over me if I'm not in charge!*), docility (*Hey! I'm no Mickey-Milquetoast!*), humility (*I've got my pride!*), and obedience (*How can I be happy if I can't do it my way?*).

Our whole society rebels against these biblically based dispositions. The opposite message is so loud and persistent that many of us have trouble hearing the truths Jesus preaches. Remember his reply to those who asked him who would be the greatest in heaven: "Whoever exalts himself will be humbled; whoever humbles himself will be exalted" (Mt 23:12).

Vastly more popular as guidelines for growth are the buzzwords of aggressiveness, self-assertion, confrontation, and empowerment. Utter self-reliance seals us off from one another: "I don't need anyone to help me." Independent self-actualization absorbs huge amounts of energy: "I have to make it on my own and be all that I can be." These are the rules of thumb in today's world.

If these sorts of demands end up being the deepest ground of our self-esteem, we will be sorely disappointed. Such self-centered motivations may lead to passing episodes of power, success, and self-congratulation. We may gain what the world considers the competitive edge, but something will be missing. That something is meekness: surrender to God's special call for our lives. This call is heard only when we listen with docility.

GRACEFUL SURRENDER

When worldly wisdom becomes the measure of our self-worth, we find it difficult to "humbly welcome the word that has been planted in [us] and is able to save [our] souls" (Jas 1:21). We may be angry at God for not giving us the graces for which we long. We may be envious of others who seem to receive more blessings than we do. Meekness helps us to value our own and others' gifts and graces. It prevents us from getting caught in the snares of harsh competition and willful imposition.

One young, happily married, successful businessman learned the value of humility only through painful experience. Having bought into the acclaim that goes with proud, self-controlled accomplishment, this man was determined to overcome by sheer ingenuity and domination all obstacles on his path to the top. Before long he would reach the pinnacle of happiness and achievement, the top of the high mountain of success reachable by only the best and the brightest.

This man soon became the young and successful president of his manufacturing company. Suddenly, out of the blue, God allowed him to be stricken like the man Job. His beloved wife fell suddenly ill. In the middle of the night, she was rushed to the hospital. The doctors could find no way to help her, and a few hours later she died. Modern medicine was unable to explain—either before or after her death—what illness had claimed this woman in the prime of life.

Her husband was stunned, speechless with grief. Shortly thereafter his brother, his most trusted confidant, became gravely ill. He, too, died a few months later. This second blow, so soon after the first devastation, was more than this success-oriented man could bear. As if all of this were not enough, the headquarters of his company, together with the adjacent factory where goods were manufactured, caught fire and exploded late one night.

In short order, all this man had built up lay in shambles. It was at that moment of feeling utterly abandoned by God that he realized—as if in a flash of faith—that he had no ultimate control over anything. He was helpless. He could not make life go the way he wanted it to, no matter how hard he tried. Neither could he "actualize" his plans and projects by his own stamina or skill alone.

From that moment on, meekness became his new companion. He knew he had no choice but to surrender to a mightier Hand, to abandon himself to the Divine Guide. He pledged to no longer build his life on the basis of his wits alone but by listening to the wisdom of God as disclosed in the Scriptures.

This man was true to his word. Instead of rushing headlong into new ventures, he began to read God's Word. As he said, "I don't drive my car any longer by myself; I let Christ drive with me and for me. He is my guide in all things. Any decision I make I discuss with him. If there is any CEO [Chief Executive Officer] in my life, it is the Lord. He's my Chairman of the Board."

Once surrendered in heart, this humbled man began to experience a turning point. Having allowed himself to be shaped and formed by divine love, he found that God gave him unexpected reserves of strength. He felt like Paul, able to execute effectively what had to be done: "I thank Christ Jesus our Lord, who has given me strength, that he considered me faithful, appointing me to his service" (1 Tm 1:12).

God led this man in due time to look for a companion for his journey who could also be a mother for his children. Within a few years, he was blessed with the gift of a deeply Christian wife with whom he has thus far enjoyed twenty-eight years of marriage. The Lord also guided him to use his remarkable business acumen to start his own company, now one of the leading businesses in the country.

Yet this successful executive has been careful not to let pride creep back into his heart. He explains his priorities to those who care to listen, from small groups to large audiences: first, to allow God to guide his life; second, to be committed to his family and to encourage them to be guided by God; and third, to pursue Christian excellence in the marketplace. As a businessman, his main model is Christ. He serves others by using the talents he has been given by God. To hear him speak and to see his demeanor is to witness what happens when a man or woman decides to enter the land of the meek.

This man's surrender brought another important benefit. Because he no longer felt compelled to manipulate events or other people, his way of dealing with everyone and everything in his life improved dramatically. As he experienced the abundant rewards of docility, he became more polite and patient with his friends, employees, and family members. He paid more attention to their thoughts and suggestions, to their stories, needs, and experiences.

The same disposition of docility extended to his style of management. It made a world of difference with colleagues, customers, and sales personnel. They all felt as if they were being treated with the utmost respect. In the past this man would have gone his own proud, self-assured way. Now he took time to appraise carefully what others had to say. He took their suggestions as possible signs of the guidance of God for his life and work.

We, too, are called to allow others—whether they are young or old, learned or simple—to be our teachers. The apostle James offered this counsel to those who would live a godly life: "Who among you is wise and understanding? Let him show his works by a good life in humility that comes from wisdom. The wisdom from above is first of all pure, then peaceable, gentle, compliant, full of mercy and good fruits, without inconstancy or insincerity" (Jas 3:13-17). Ask yourself: *Do I follow Jesus' example? Or am I com - pelled to have the last word? Am I responsive to people who exemplify a meeker style of life? Or do I tend to follow a more "macho" way?*

BLESSINGS OF SILENT SURRENDER

Growth in spiritual maturity does not usually produce such startling results. We more often experience a few "barely noticeable improvements." Yet without meekness, we can neither receive direction from the Holy Spirit nor give good guidance in God's name to those entrusted to our care.

We may strive to put into practice the scriptural admonition, "Exalt not yourself lest you fall and bring upon you dishonor" (Sir 1:27). We may notice ourselves being less driven by anger, less pushed by pretenses of power. We may even feel like we're letting go of our make-believe self-importance. We stop taking pride in how much better or smarter or greater in God's eyes we are than others. We begin to feel pretty good about ourselves. The Pharisee in us doesn't have a leg to stand on!

Thanks to the lessons life teaches, we learn more about how limited we are. Every time we become puffed up by our own importance, we are bound to be disappointed. Our predictions never match the reality God wants to disclose to us. Pride of mastery obscures meekness. It veils the guiding grace of God, whereas docility releases it.

At times we may have to put our opinions on the back burner. Whether this decision is cowardly or wise depends on why we do it. You can examine your motives by asking yourself a few revealing questions. *Do I refuse to speak up because I am afraid of what others may think of me? What if they fail to accord me the honor I secretly long to receive? Do I withdraw in anxious silence for the wrong reasons?*

The choice to remain silent may be a response to the prompting of grace. The time may not be right to proclaim what we believe. We may have to be patient for a while. If we express our opinions too forcefully or prematurely, we may incur swift rejection. Our manner of communication may threaten or hurt those we're trying to reach.

At such moments of indecisiveness, God may give us the wisdom and courage to bear with ambiguity, to wait upon his guidance in holy patience. At the opportune time, we will know what to say and do in Christ's name. Good results are brought about by his grace, not our own doing.

Docile Christians try to act and speak with prudence rather than being obnoxious, pushy, insensitive, or sentimental. Inspired by Jesus and Mary, by saintly disciples of all ages, they make an effort to balance gentleness with firmness, meekness with boldness. They try to keep destructive anger in check while using the energy behind this emotion to find creative solutions to life's problems.

Once we accept the fact that nothing is perfect, we will be less inclined to throw up our hands in exasperation, or to give up in irritation because things do not go our way or because we can never reach perfection here on earth. The venerable Francis Libermann (1802-1852), one of France's great spiritual masters, counseled his missionaries in how to deal with imperfection:

> It is... important to know how to be flexible, how to adjust and accommodate ourselves to... people, things, and circumstances.... We are right in wanting to see everything done perfectly.... But we may as well make up our minds that we will encounter imperfection wherever we encounter human beings. Let us try to achieve the maximum, but let's not break anything in the process. Otherwise, we lose twenty times more than we gain and in the end, if we're honest, we'll soon realize that we are rather far from being perfect ourselves because we demand such absolute perfection of others. I have observed that the really great saints always acted in the way I have recommended. Only the "petty" saints, the ones who haven't gone very far along the road of piety, act contrariwise.[1]

To put it another way, we cannot expect to change the course of every river. We have to be content when we are carried firmly yet gently by the mighty current of God's guiding grace. What we most need at times is to let go, to relax and float in the sea of our Divine Guide. The God in whose likeness we have been made (Gn 1:26) will carry us along in love. Jesus will give us the courage we need to tackle our troubles. He will help us to go on with our lives.

Francis Libermann felt this way. He emphasized the right balance between determination and docility: "If we are able to force consciences to be pure, wills to be good, and minds to be truthful, it is evident that we should do so. Charity would make it our duty. But there is no one in this world who can even slightly force the consciences, wills, or minds of his fellowmen. God didn't want to do it. Why should we?"[2]

MATURING IN GENTLENESS AND FIRMNESS[3]

We can learn much from a spiritual master known for his docile demeanor: the renowned seventeenth-century French spiritual director, bishop, and canonized saint, Francis de Sales (1567-1622). His call to the devout life is as relevant today as when he first issued it:

> Lift up your heart... whenever it falls, but do so meekly by humbling yourself before God through knowledge of your own misery and do not be surprised if you fall. It is no wonder that infirmity should be infirm, weakness weak, or misery wretched. Nevertheless, detest with all your powers the offense God has received from you and with great courage and confidence in his mercy return to the path of virtue you had forsaken.[4]

In his acknowledged Christian classic, *Introduction to the Devout Life*, St. Francis de Sales alludes to the interplay of meekness and determination: "If we are proud, puffed up, and enraged when we are stung and bitten by detractors and enemies, it is a sure sign that in us neither humility nor meekness is genuine and sincere but only apparent and artificial."[5]

Who of us has not been distressed when we hear directly or "by the grapevine" that someone has said something less than complimentary about us—especially when the detraction isn't even true? If there is ever a time when we want nothing to do with meekness, it is when we are the victim of a lie. We feel enraged about the injustice. We know we don't deserve such treatment, not even from an "enemy."

An angry desire to strike back can flash through us so spontaneously that we may not be able to do much to hinder it. This initial inner explosion is a sure sign that we have been "stung," that our flesh is alive and well. We incur no guilt because of it. The burden of proof resides not in our automatic reaction but in our free response to the feeling aroused in us.

If, under the guidance of God, the virtue of docility has matured in us, we will be able to douse the fires of our initial reaction and properly assess the situation. The first step is to regain perspective by placing our hurt, indignant feelings in the light of faith. We remind ourselves that God may use criticism, however harsh or unfair it may be, to deepen our humility. He may use it to guide us to new insights into how we can improve the ways we relate to others.

Anything that happens to us is meant to purify our sensual and spiritual self-centeredness. We can take this sting for what it is—a reminder of the imperfection of the human condition—and make of it an invitation to identify with the crucified Christ. For this reason, St. Francis goes on to say: "We must not be angry with one another on the way, but rather we must march on as a band of... companions united in meekness, peace, and love. I state absolutely and make no exception, do not be angry at all if that is possible. Do not accept any pretext whatever for opening your heart's door to anger."[6]

What can St. Francis mean when he says that we must not open our heart's door to anger? Humanly speaking, that seems impossible. This spiritual master is counseling us to watch lest our hearts become overwhelmed by rage running out of control.

Knowing that anger can get away from us before we know it, he offers an antidote to the swift-acting poison of rage: to make an "act of meekness" toward the person or persons who pressured us into losing our "cool." St. Francis counsels: "So also we must repair our anger instantly by a contrary act of meekness. Fresh wounds are quickest healed, as the saying goes."[7]

This might mean backing away from a tense situation until we calm down. Perhaps we have to approach the person who made us angry and ask for an occasion to talk things over. What we can always do is to turn to our Divine Guide for help. We can pray for peace within our hearts as well as for the person who hurt us. Perhaps God will provide an opening to settle our differences.

We need to change the course of our anger rather than bury it. Buried rage may do us more harm than would venting it on the one who made us so mad. Anger can harden our hearts, paralyzing our genuine will to show love toward someone if we cannot feel that love. St. Francis reminds us that we ourselves are the greatest beneficiaries of meekness. When we become God-molded persons, we no longer "fret over our own imperfections"[8]—especially over spontaneous, and at times uncontrollable, upsurges of anger. What counts is our healing response.

Even if we give in to anger on occasion, it is never too late to change. The grace of God will guide us out of our destructive mood and enable us to channel that energy in a positive direction. Through spiritual reading of Scripture and the masters, we will see how necessary it is to boldly pursue reconciliation and make a new start.

To mature over a lifetime in the wisdom of this beatitude, we must trust that the Lord is leading us at every moment. If we want to enter the land of divine likeness, we must allow the Holy Spirit to calm our perturbed spirits whenever willfulness gets in the way of listening to God. To imitate our Divine Guide, we should try to become at the same time meek and bold.

Gentleness, called the "flower of charity" by St. Bernard of Clairvaux, awakens us to follow the God of love rather than any other master. Let another excellent guide, St. Teresa of Avila, have the last word: "I give you one counsel: that you don't think that through your own strength or efforts you can arrive, for reaching this stage is beyond our power; if you try to reach it, the devotion you have will grow cold. But with simplicity and humility, which will achieve everything, say: [Thy will be done]."[9]

TIME TO REFLECT

Now is the time to consider what pushes your buttons. What makes you fail to practice docility? On the other hand, what prompts you to become more Christlike in any given situation? Carefully consider how the following counsels apply to your life.

1. Place the Christ who is gentle and humble of heart at the center of your life. If Jesus were standing beside you, would you continue to be defensive, angry, or willful?

2. Treat your limits not only as hurdles to cross but as graced openings to the guidance of God. Open your ears to hear the lessons to be learned from failure.

3. Do not let silent surrender be an insult to your pride. Instead, see humble submission as a way to imitate your Redeemer's docility. What matters most is what's going on in your heart, not how other people view your actions.

4. Do not be too quick to view the mistreatment of others as threatening. Guard against becoming overly self-defensive. Learn to listen to both compliments and criticisms with equanimity and good humor.

5. Do not feel bound to have the last word. Listen with humility to your teachers just as Jesus did when he went with his parents to Nazareth and "was obedient to them" (Lk 2:51).

6. Try to see with meek and mild eyes treasures of meaning in troublesome situations. Replace anger with appreciation as often as you can.

7. Acknowledge your anger lest it leak out in cutting remarks or subtle insinuations. A slush fund of anger will one day explode—in you and onto others.

8. Let your Divine Guide show you how to balance dominance with docility.

9. Quell your need to follow the crowd. Focus instead on what gives glory to God.

10. Pray for the grace of meekness. Let it clothe you with "heartfelt compassion, kindness, humility, gentleness, and patience" (Col 3:12).

MEEKNESS OF HEART
Adrian van Kaam

Lord,
You want me to learn from you
Meekness of heart.
No matter how I fail you,
Your meekness makes me trust in you.
You are slow to anger;
Your kindness is without limit.
You tell me not to be distressed,
To let your meekness be my own,
Finding rest in you alone.

Give me the wisdom to make time each day
For a gentle nursing of my soul.
Free me from arrogance,
From goals too sublime for me.
Still and quiet my soul
As a mother quiets the little one on her lap.
Free me from the need for achievement.
Make my life less forceful, more gentle,
Centered in you alone.

Let the splendor of your presence
Light up my everydayness.
Make me a smooth channel for the outflow
Of your Divine Will in this world.
Let me dwell meekly
In the presence of your Mystery.
Harmonize my frail spirit with the infinite Spirit
Who fills the universe and its history.

Jesus, holy, meek, and mild
Make my heart less harsh and wild,
Melt away its stubborn pride.

CHAPTER NINE

Peace Anchors Us in the Divine Family

Blessed are the peacemakers; they shall
be called children of God.   **Matthew 5:9**

The eighth guideline to divine guidance echoes the words
of Jesus: *Make peace.*

As we grow in oneness with the Prince of Peace, we may sense
an inner harmony not of our own making. Raging storms grow
calm. Relationships improve. Irritation gives way to relaxation,
tension to contentment. Whereas we used to rush headlong into
every invitation or event, we now take time to enjoy the present
moment.

Without this internal harbor of tranquility, we cannot become
peacemakers. Simply put, we cannot share with others what we
have not received ourselves.

Peace was the Lord's farewell gift to his disciples: "Peace I leave
with you; my peace I give to you. Not as the world gives do I give
it to you. Do not let your hearts be troubled or afraid" (Jn 14:27).
Jesus' choice of farewell gifts tells us that his peace is precious
beyond price, and that it cannot be attained by our own power.

We know from experience that our lives are often too scattered
and distracted to be at peace. Input from the media bombards us;

duties and responsibilities pull us in many different directions at once. We quickly lose our center. Then, when we least expect it, the peace of Christ that surpasses understanding may enter our hearts (Phil 4:7). If we ourselves are at peace, those around us feel it. People want to be with us. They sense about us an aura or presence difficult to define but definitely real.

Without understanding why, others respond to the peace that emanates from those who follow Christ. By the working of the Holy Spirit, we enter into an ongoing process of transformation. Our life of prayer and participation grows more consonant with the grace and goodness of our Divine Guide. As beloved sons and daughters of the Father, we enjoy a nearness to the source of peace no inner turmoil or outer conflict can destroy.

STRIKING A BALANCE

This profound gift of inner peace ought not to be mistaken for a passive attitude of apathy and indifference. Neither must we believe that Jesus wants us to make peace at any price. Both are extreme postures. The one refuses to do anything to foster peace; the other tries to do too much at the risk of compromising Christian truths and values.

How can we strike the right note of balance? On the one hand, we pray for the grace of appreciative abandonment to the mystery, for acceptance of what is. For example, we may have to live with someone who suffers the disease of alcoholism, with a chronically sick child, with a dreary job done out of the necessity to support a family. On the other hand, we pray for the grace to meet the challenge to do something—to attend Alanon meetings regularly, to seek medical advice, to look for a feasible retraining program. We seek through prayer to know when we are veering too far in the direction of either passivity or hyperactivity.

Just as meekness means both docility and determination, so peace connotes both trust and tenacity. We trust that the Holy Spirit will guide us as we try to give form to the best possible conditions for a peaceful life. We pray for the grace to recognize and stay with what is given to us from the guiding Hand of God. And we ask for tenacity in our attempts to change in ourselves what goes against our resolve to be faithful to Christ's call.

Peacemaking is somewhat of a balancing act. Only when we live in the peace given to us by Jesus can we begin to practice what is both an art and a discipline. We have to be willing to lay our lives on the line, to take some initiative while still remaining humble instruments of the Prince of Peace.

Contrary to the cultural stereotype, peacemakers are not laidback people. They know how to take responsibility within their own sphere of influence. Some are called to save the environment—to make peace with nature, so to speak. Others are drawn to look for ways to actively relieve the plight of the disadvantaged. In other words, peacemaking implies the task of creating a just society within the limits and possibilities given to us.

Peacemaking in Christ's name is inseparable from social justice and mercy. All three come together in a Christian vision of what society should be. Every effort ought to be made to improve relationships between people, to show benevolence, to be companions on the way. Peacemaking inspires us to do what we can to mitigate the rage and resentment that prevent people from acknowledging that they are brothers and sisters of Jesus, sons and daughters of the same caring Father.

The gift of peace is so wonderful that we aren't able to keep it for ourselves. We want to share it with others. It sorely needs to be spread far and wide in a violent, war-torn world like our own. What a mockery it would be to proclaim the importance of peace and not do anything to make it a reality.

A good place to start this peace process is around the family dinner table. There we must take the first steps toward creating peace in our world. When siblings stop bickering, when spouses make love instead of war, when believers stop being Christian in name only and make Christ their role model, they may find that peacemaking is no longer such an unreachable goal.

Paul captures this peace-filled vision in his Second Letter to Timothy. He calls those led by the Lord to turn from the dominance of unillumined passions and to pursue instead righteousness, faith, love, and peace (2 Tm 2:22). He then spells out in detail what it means to share Christ's peace with others. We need to read these words with reverence and take them to heart if we want to be peacemakers:

> Avoid foolish and ignorant debates, for you know that they breed quarrels. A [servant] of the Lord should not quarrel, but should be gentle with everyone, able to teach, tolerant, correcting opponents with kindness. It may be that God will grant them repentance that leads to knowledge of the truth, and that they may return to their senses out of the devil's snare, where they are entrapped by him, for his will.   2 Timothy 2:23-26

PRACTICAL STEPS TO PEACEMAKING

Being peacemakers requires that we take decisive steps. We will use the experience of a woman named Michelle to understand what these steps entail.

First, peacemaking begins with becoming more sensitive to the moments and occasions when you lose inner peace. Michelle's days are too full, and she knows it. Peace eludes her like a bird on the wing. She wants to recapture the feeling of serenity she once knew, but her daily rounds exhaust her, and her nights bring no rest. Does her plight sound at all familiar?

Michelle takes the first step necessary to restore inner peace by admitting its absence. She decides to tune in to God's pace, to slow down and listen to the still small whisper of his guidance in daily events. A just-noticeable improvement occurs. Her short fuse lengthens! Her patience increases. Michelle no longer creates around her a climate of depletion and depreciation—the all-too-common outcomes of lost peace.

What signs indicate to her that inner peace is on the rise? She notices the diminishing swings between valleys of depression and peaks of elation, with no rest in between. Her moods become more even; her equanimity and tranquility return. Others notice the difference and commend Michelle for her increased serenity.

Second, let the inner peace you feel spread to the outer world. The environment at home convinced Michelle that she had to change. She could no longer stand the climate of constant bickering. Once she decided to alter her own course, things improved visibly. Her calmness soothed testy children and happily surprised her spouse. Her two boys stopped using each other as whipping posts when Michelle's fights with her husband became less frequent.

These changes soon spread beyond her own family. Her colleagues at work knew Michelle was different because she would no longer tolerate making others the brunt of cynical jokes. She sought to work out disagreements rather than let them trigger hostile arguments. She kept her occasionally irascible temperament in check.

Perceiving Michelle as an effective peacemaker, her coworkers began to seek her out when divisive or disruptive issues arose. Her serene presence was like an anchor in a stormy sea. What was her secret? It lay in the third decisive step to peacemaking.

Last but not least, keep the Prince of Peace at your side. Michelle knew she could be neither a woman of peace nor a peacemaker based on her own power. Throughout her quest for inner harmony and outer composure, she sought divine guidance. She purposefully took time to rest in God and seek the way of peace taught by Jesus.

Michelle knew that without the Prince of Peace at her side, her best efforts at peacemaking would only backfire. In the past, when her world was spinning out of control, when she felt as if she had reached the end of her rope, she had tried foolishly to pull her own life together. Michelle desperately wanted peace. She sincerely wanted to be a peacemaker. But she had forgotten to pray. Now she gladly admits she can do none of this without God's help.

With the Spirit of Jesus as her guide, Michelle stops making excuses for inner agitation and quickly investigates what might be causing her unrest. She then returns to the place of calm from which she departed and resets her course. She clings to Christ, like a person lost at sea holds on to a raft for dear life. She thereby makes herself available—should the Lord choose to use her—to make peace.

Such honesty with ourselves and others is the key to lasting peace. Putting these steps into practice allows us to seek creative ways of turning conflicts into occasions for peacemaking. We quit trying to force others to fit into a world that suits us. We stop imposing on them demands they find impossible to fulfill.

Inner peace provides fertile ground for the flowering of patience. We find ourselves better able to keep flare-ups in check before they explode into full-blown fireworks. Our growing sensitivity enables us to find peaceful solutions to problems that would otherwise lead to more violence in an already disjointed world. By means of his farewell gift, Christ makes possible a better way.

THE FRUIT OF PEACE

Peacemaking can be effective only under the guidance of the Holy Spirit. We need the gifts of wisdom, counsel, and fear of the Lord, along with the cardinal virtues of prudence, justice, fortitude, and temperance. Without these cornerstones of personal formation and communal harmony, we cannot hope to fulfill the exhortations of the apostle Paul: "Be at peace among yourselves... admonish the idle; cheer the fainthearted; support the weak; be patient with all. See that no one returns evil for evil; rather, always seek what is good for each other and for all" (1 Thes 5:13-15).

St. Catherine of Siena (1347-1380) exemplifies this text. This fourteenth-century master of the spiritual life is a teacher of the truth and a reliable channel of God's spiritual guidance. St. Catherine also proved to be a noteworthy peacemaker in the midst of turbulent times, especially in negotiating the return of the papacy to Rome during the Avignon controversy.

Her *Dialogue* records the conversations with Christ that guided her life of peace and her peacemaking. Peace of this sort signifies that we are at home in the Trinity. God is a "peaceful sea," and we are immersed in it, drawn ever more closely by grace to the "eternal Godhead."

To feel oneself in the presence of the Holy "brings the soul to such joy and spiritual peace that no tongue can describe it."[1] The soul becomes more at one with God's will, with God's Word, Christ crucified, and with the Holy Spirit. Catherine goes on to say that this presence in us nourishes the fruit of peace, "true patience."[2]

For Catherine, the mark of having merited the name "children of God" is to image the Trinity. Our created being then radiates the love that made us, the hope that saves us, and the faith that leads us through the darkest nights. Thus says the Father: "Get up, then, and follow [Jesus] for no one can come to me, the Father, except through him. He is the way and the gate through whom you must enter into me, the sea of peace."[3]

What happens to those who immerse themselves in this sea? Catherine gives the answer: "They are always peaceful and calm, and nothing can scandalize them because they have done away with what causes them to take scandal, their self-will."[4]

Here, then, are the first fruits of being peacemakers. Where others may be in a frenzy over some ultimately unimportant problem, we try to remain calm. When scandalous things happen, as they certainly did in Catherine's time, we do not allow ourselves to be so offended that we lose our peace.

How is this possible? Only by surrendering our self-will to God, doing what we can to remedy the situation, and leaving the final outcome in God's hands. Thus positioned, we are less apt to forfeit our peace when people persecute us, or demons hound us, or temptations wash over us. Difficult times become occasions to anchor our imperiled ship by means of the rope Christ provides when we call out to him for help.

Spiritual masters agree on a sure sign indicating those who are living in tune with the Holy Spirit and hence guided by God: peace combined with "joy in everything." As Catherine is told by the Lord: "They find joy in everything. They do not sit in judgment on my servants or anyone else, but rejoice in every situation and every way of living they see, saying 'Thanks to you, eternal Father, that in your house there are so many dwelling places!'"[5]

Joy accompanies peace when we give up trying to judge every person and situation on our own terms. Only then can we rejoice in the lavish abundance of God's gifts to so many unique people. Why would we want to make war with anyone else in such an atmosphere of appreciation? Peace is thus inseparable from joy in hearts guided by God.

WE SHALL BE CALLED THE CHILDREN OF GOD

When St. Catherine received the Eucharist, she lived to the full the farewell gift of Jesus. Quoting his words to her, she writes: "Just as the fish is in the sea and the sea in the fish, so am I in the soul and the soul in me, the sea of peace."[6]

What a wonderful image this is. If God is a sea of peace and we are "fish" immersed in that sea, then we want to stay close to him who gives us life. We do not want to be flung onto the shore and left gasping for breath. We want to receive the blessing given to those who are peacemakers: being called the children of God.

St. Thérèse of Lisieux saw herself in a special way as a child of God.[7] One day little Thérèse asked her older sister, Celine, to explain to her the mystery of grace. Rather than confuse the child with a lot of theology, Celine told her sister to fetch a tumbler from the kitchen and a thimble from the sewing room. Being a good teacher, she turned her little sister's question into a game.

When Thérèse returned with the vessels in hand, Celine said to her, "Go and fill each one with as much water as it can hold." After the little saint had done as she was told, her older sister asked her, "Now, Thérèse, observe well, which of these two vessels is the fullest?"

The child studied both of them and concluded rightly, "Both are just as full."

"And so it is," said Celine, "with God's grace. He fills each of us to the fullest capacity. Some may be tumblers, some may be thimbles, but all of us have a special place in the divine plan." St. Thérèse herself proved to be one of the larger tumblers into whom God poured a great portion of his sea of grace.

Anyone who has been adopted into the divine family can be immersed in this sea of peace and filled by this sea of grace. As we enter into this intimate union of love, we must be willing to shed the shackles of sensual or spiritual self-centeredness along with all their disruptive traces. We take refuge in the peaceful harbor of the Trinity whenever we feel engulfed by any storm.

When we do feel tempest-tossed, Christ will be at our side as he was with the disciples on the Sea of Galilee (Lk 8:22-25). He will calm the wind and the waves; he will protect us from the troubles and temptations that threaten to destroy our peace and joy.

Blessed are the peacemakers; they shall be called children of God, those who share in the eternal circle of consonance that binds Father, Son, and Holy Spirit in trinitarian splendor.

TIME TO REFLECT

Do you want to live as children of God? If the answer is a resounding yes, then you must be willing to identify and overcome barriers to peace in your own heart. Ask yourself: *What must I do, in response to the guidance of God, to be worthy to receive the gift of "perfect blessedness"?*[8] The following counsels can help you to become a peace-filled person, as well as a carrier of peace to others.

1. Rather than living by the dictates of your own willful pride, seek to put on the mind and heart of Jesus. Consider how he would handle a particular situation that has you baffled or ruffled.

2. When you lose your peace, don't be discouraged. When your life is shattered by circumstances beyond your control, dive headlong into the sea of peace and God will catch you.

3. Remember that you cannot find peace and joy in what is passing. Neither can you achieve it on your own. Lasting peace can be yours only when you rest in the ocean of divine peace: God himself.

4. Do not expect to find peace in humanistically based peace movements unless you have found peace in your own heart first.

5. Never seek peace at any price if it means betraying your call or, worse still, suppressing the rights of others to seek and find their own God-guided destiny.

6. Appraise as possible signs of God's guidance the messages of peace that come to you in your daily life with others.

7. Try to see that the gift of peace means far more than the cessation of conflict or the absence of trouble. True peace calls for continual growth in inner and outer consonance with God, self, and others.

8. See adversity not only as a danger but as an opportunity for making peace in tune with and through the source of peace, Christ within you.[9]

9. Believe with your whole heart in God's promise of a coming reign of peace. Only in the presence of the Prince of Peace (Is 9:5) can we find the harmony we seek.

10. Even though peace in our world seems to be an impossible dream, don't lose hope. Turn to Jesus. Ask him to uproot injustice, to plant seeds of mercy that will heal the human race.

PRIESTLY PRAYER OF PEACE
Adrian van Kaam

Priestly prayer of the Lord,
Joyful word of adoration,
Saying thanks in an oblation
Of human life,
Song of peace, of aspiration,
Consecrating everything
We say and do.

Priestly prayer,
Rising softly
From your likeness in the soul
Released into our longing heart,
Pervading life with serenity
And sweet surrender.

Priestly prayer,
Healing self-despisal
That unexpected failure
Breeds in excited minds,
Winding down
Into the chambers of anxiety
That imprison potencies for peace.

Priestly prayer,
Slaying foolish pride,
Poison of humanity, source of war,
Mother of cruelty and subtle slander,
Blight on the serenity we seek.

O let your priestly prayer
Lift degraded life
To a festive prayer of peace
In the midst of persecution
By the Evil One.

CHAPTER TEN

Poverty: Depending on God for Everything

Blessed are the poor in spirit; the kingdom of heaven is theirs. **Matthew 5:3**

The ninth guideline to divine guidance can be formulated in this way: *Depend on God for everything.*

A story told of a young boy from a well-to-do family illustrates this principle. One day the carefree youth climbed a tree, found a sturdy branch, and swung his knees over it. With his head hanging down like a pendant, the lad had a sudden revelation of the entire human race. He saw all of us, himself included, as literally dangling from God, utterly dependent on his strength to keep us from falling into oblivion. This boy came to be known as St. Francis of Assisi.

When we are well off, as the young Francis was, we tend not to think along these lines. But shifting the scene to more desperate circumstances erases any lingering doubt from our minds. We see at a glance that we are totally reliant on God's help. We could not get through a single day without it, much less negotiate the stiff demands of a lifetime.

An immigrant from Argentina who lives in our neighborhood

came to America without a penny in his pocket. But Santos had a dream: to become a citizen and an honest wage earner. He knew such a life would require stamina, courage, and the kind of faith that can move mountains. Santos said that his mother's words of farewell were seared on his heart like a cattle brand: "My son, work as if everything depended on you, but remember that everything you do depends on God."

This old saying gave him hope when he did menial chores for minimum wage. Everything was scarce, but Santos was an excellent gardener and the provisions came. He was poor for a good many years but rich in what counted: the faith of his people. No hardship could prevent him from holding on to God. Santos spread his arms in a gesture of gratitude and said to us, as if he were the master of all he surveyed, "My mother was a wise woman. The more I depend on God for everything, the more he provides."

DO YOU OWN YOUR POSSESSIONS— OR DO THEY OWN YOU?

Ask yourself what might be keeping you from depending more on God: *Is my mind too crammed with ideas or my heart too consumed by other desires? Am I too possessed by my possessions to acknowledge my need for God and to thank him for every breath I breathe? Am I too persuaded of my own importance or too confident of my own resources? Or, on the other end of the pendulum, do I feel so hopeless about some personal difficulty that I see myself as beyond God's reach?*

When we meditate on the life of Jesus, we may get an inkling of how bound we are to our possessions (houses, jewelry, cars, clothing). We easily forget to view them not as gifts of God but as ends in themselves. Other sources of inordinate attachment tempt us too—such things as status, worldly success, upward mobility, and the ever-present and dangerous love of money that St. Paul rightly names the root of all evil (1 Tm 6:10).

Release from such bondage is not something we can manage alone. It is only in and through Christ that we can keep the things of this world in their proper perspective. In contrast to the personal deprivation Jesus freely embraced, we begin to see more clearly how frequently we seek our own gratification.

Picture the glorious Son of God, reduced to the status of a criminal with nothing more to show for his years of labor than a tattered cloak and a crown of thorns. He was nailed to a cross for our sake. All too often we are figuratively nailed to what we own or control. He makes us think about how tied we are to what is less than lasting. As Scripture says, what good would it do to gain the whole world and to lose our soul in the process? (Mt 16:26). Christ's selfless desire to save us teaches us a powerful lesson in letting go.

When Peter asked whether or not they should pay their taxes, Jesus literally told him to go fishing. This seasoned fisherman did as he was told: Peter went down to the lake, grabbed the first fish he saw, and pulled two coins out of its mouth—one for his tax and one for the Lord's. Jesus makes the point that we are to render to Caesar what is Caesar's and to God what is God's (Mk 12:17). He wants us to see the difference between merely owning things and using them wisely for the greater glory of God and in thanksgiving for his gifts.

The gift of spiritual poverty guards us from becoming enslaved to an abundance of material goods, but it also accomplishes a much deeper work. It produces a unitive disposition of the heart and opens us to any guiding message the Holy Spirit may want to communicate. When we live this beatitude in imitation of Christ, we develop a healthier appreciation of the real but limited value of people, events, and things in and by themselves alone.

As we become more convinced of our absolute indigence and dependence on God, we become more receptive to the graces flowing into us from the life of the Trinity. The gift of spiritual poverty produces profound gratitude that Jesus suffered for our sake, we who are not worthy to buckle his sandals. "God proves his love for us in that while we were still sinners Christ died for us.... Not only that, but we also boast of God through our Lord Jesus Christ, through whom we have now received reconciliation" (Rom 5:8-11).

Receiving this gift of divine love helps us to become detached from anything less than God as the ultimate meaning and aim of our lives. Adoration of Christ, who emptied himself for our sake, fills us to overflowing with faith, hope, and love. And love takes away the blinders that keep us from seeing inner poverty as the path to empowerment by the Holy Spirit.

EMPTYING OURSELVES IN IMITATION OF CHRIST

Poverty of spirit also readies us to be generous toward others. If God could love us enough to send his only begotten Son to save us, can we not share what we have with those less fortunate? The widow who gave her last mite held on to nothing (Lk 21:4). We, too, have to give from the heart. Even when someone takes advantage of our generosity, we should not be surprised to receive a hundredfold in return (Lk 8:8).

When we strive to imitate the self-emptying Christ, we allow the poor to become our teachers. Gail was a nurse who specialized in the care of the terminally ill. She had been doing this work at hospitals and in hospices for many years. When we met her, Gail laughed when we asked "the same question I have had to answer so many times I feel like a broken record." We wanted to know how she found the strength to maintain her faith and good cheer.

Gail said simply, "I'm no heroine. I do this work because I receive more from my patients than I could give them in *two* lifetimes. It is a privilege to see in such poverty the outpouring of a thousand graces. I witness daily the relinquishment of everything the rest of us hold on to for dear life. I do not need to look up the definition of detachment in the dictionary. My patients are the best spiritual teachers I know."

Gail's words touched us deeply. We knew what a privileged person she was when she added softly: "You see, I am at the bedside of Jesus."

Our Lord "did not regard equality with God something to be grasped.... He emptied himself, taking the form of a slave, coming in human likeness" (Phil 2:6-7). Jesus the man is like us in all things but sin. He is the perfect model of the paradox that renunciation leads to liberation from avarice and greed.

Jesus underscores the message of this beatitude in many of his stories: the rich young man (Mt 19:16-22); the rich man and the steward (Lk 16:1-13); the rich man and Lazarus (Lk 16:19-31). He teaches us also by personal example: his birth in a manger (Lk 2:7); his hidden life in Nazareth (Lk 2:39); his final agony (Lk 23:44-46).

Jesus dined with the destitute because they were not filled with the fare of their own self-importance. They could listen to his message because they were free from the pressures of worldly affairs. They heeded his advice not to cling to purses that wear out, but to seek "an inexhaustible treasure in heaven that no thief can reach nor moth destroy. For where your treasure is, there also will your heart be" (Lk 12:33-34).

What a joy it must have been for these little ones in the eyes of the world to hear words that rang true to their experience. Jesus assured them that they would not find lasting treasure in grass that grows today and tomorrow is thrown into the fire (Mt 6:30).

Through the words and example of Christ, God clearly calls us to care for all the poor. Jesus speaks on behalf of those who are unjustly deprived of material goods—widows, orphans, migrant laborers, the children of crack addicts. He also answers the prayers of the centurion (Mt 8:5-13), the request of a synagogue leader (Lk 8:40-56), and the pleading of a tax collector named Zacchaeus (Lk 19:1-10).

Jesus also wants us to address the needs of the *spiritually* poor like Nicodemus and the Samaritan woman. And he speaks to the rich on the right use of money (Lk 16:9-15). By mingling with both the indigent and the well-to-do, the Lord teaches us that all people stand in need of his love and guidance. Thus he sends generous servants to all areas of need: artists to care for the aesthetically deprived; medical researchers to discover new ways to help the physically disabled; creative employers to put whole neighborhoods back to work.

The desires of the poor and the rich may differ on the scale of material and spiritual poverty, but everyone has needs. All people suffer from some form of inner and outer deprivation. No one can escape the limits of the human condition.

POVERTY OF SPIRIT OPENS US TO DIVINE GUIDANCE

Acknowledging our dependency on God quiets the tempests stirred up by grandiose claims to self-reliance and worldly self-esteem. An "I-can-do-it-alone" mentality puffs us up with feelings of superiority like helium-filled balloons. It may also cover up our reluctance to be transparent before others for fear of rejection. The least prick of criticism and we burst.

Jesus did not take the sin of pride lightly: "Woe to you, scribes and Pharisees, you frauds. You cleanse the outside of cup and dish, but leave the inside full of loot and lust.... You are like whitewashed tombs, beautiful to look at on the outside but inside full of filth and dead men's bones" (Mt 23:25-27).

Jesus addressed the spiritual leaders of his day as "blind guides, who strain out the gnat and swallow the camel!" (Mt 23:24). Imposition of our own will instead of the will of God results in mis-direction—for which we, like the Pharisees, are held responsible. The poor in spirit, by contrast, let the Holy Spirit guide them with their humble and detached cooperation. They let God take the ini-tiative *and* do the leading.

Refusing to embrace spiritual poverty places us at great risk of missing the mark. Once we adopt the posture of self-important, omniscient guides, we lose the awareness that the light we are to fol-low comes to us as a gift of grace. Wisdom is neither a product of human cleverness nor a byproduct of a secret need to control others.

Whether we seek guidance directly from the Holy Spirit or ask questions of a qualified guide, what we most need is freedom from hypocrisy. Without the gifts of poverty of spirit and inner detachment, no self-declared director of souls can be trusted. Such a person's intention, like that of a blacksmith (a favorite image of St. John of the Cross), is to hammer us into the shape he or she thinks is God's will for us.

In poverty of spirit, we become servants of those who ask us for guidance. We try like artists to draw out the unique image of God in which these individuals were originally created and are now continually being formed. "All of us, gazing with unveiled face on the glory of the Lord, are being transformed into the same image from glory to glory, as from the Lord who is the Spirit" (2 Cor 3:18).

Poverty of spirit means being content to seek God's will over a lifetime. We must be patient with our mistakes, when we misread the direction in which we or others are to go. God is bigger than our errors in judgment or our detours on the road. The goal we seek—union with the Trinity—is not a badge of merit but a blessing bestowed upon us by a generous lover of souls.

TWO LOVERS OF LADY POVERTY

The importance of this beatitude cannot be underestimated for the purposes of divine guidance. Poverty is the opposite of pride. Pride shuts us off from God's guiding light. It turns us into prisoners of the Prince of Darkness (Col 1:13). That is why a master of the spiritual life like Francis of Assisi (1182-1226) advises us to embrace Lady Poverty before any other gift.

The life of St. Francis witnesses to the truth that such poverty is not a matter of saying voluminous prayers, doing stacks of good deeds, or fasting excessively. In the following words, he speaks directly about this beatitude:

There are many who, applying themselves insistently to prayers and good deeds, engage in much abstinence and many mortifications of their bodies, but they are scandalized and quickly roused to anger by a single word which seems injurious to their person, or by some other things which might be taken from them. These [persons] are not poor in spirit because a person who is truly poor in spirit hates himself (Lk 14:26) and loves those who strike him on the cheek (Mt 5:39).[1]

Worthwhile as mortification may be in moderation, neither material deprivation nor disciplines like abstinence lead in themselves to poverty of spirit. After fasting all day, we foolishly imagine that we have emptied ourselves and become self-giving. Then why do we turn around and become irritable when someone takes something we own without our permission?

Francis is not naive about empty posturings of poverty. For him the test comes when we begin to "hate" anything in us that makes us proud or that prevents us from imitating the generosity of Jesus. To put it another way, we grow poor in spirit when we begin to "love" opportunities in which we can undergo with the suffering Christ the purgation of our pride, when we allow our enemies to strike us on the cheek. Only then can we say with humility that perhaps we are growing in the spirit of poverty, and therewith in our ability to appraise the will of God.

Clare of Assisi (1194-1253) agrees with Francis. She says that only when we recognize our "absolute need" can we enjoy to the full "heavenly nourishment."[2] When she prays in poverty of spirit, a sense of awe overtakes her. Thus she sings:

O blessed poverty,
    who bestows eternal riches
    on those who love and embrace her!

O holy poverty,
    to those who possess and desire you
God promises the kingdom of heaven
    and offers, indeed, eternal glory and blessed life![3]

Clare perceived poverty of spirit and God-centeredness as one and the same. She lived by the truth that "the kingdom of heaven is promised and given by the Lord only to the poor."[4] Anyone who loves temporal things more than the Eternal who made them, according to Clare, loses the fruit of love. Both she and Francis accepted without any doubt Jesus' teaching that we cannot serve two masters, God and money, for we will either love the one and hate the other or serve the one and despise the other (Mt 6:24).

As we learn to attach ourselves more firmly to the source of lasting treasures, we begin to see each finite aspect of our lives as a manifestation of God's infinite care. Along with saints such as Francis and Clare, we become more mindful of our own nothingness and God's allness. Whenever we are tempted to grow arrogant, we try to allow the loving witness of the Lord to lift the veil of self-deception from our eyes.

In short, we begin to rely on God alone. Only then can we enter his kingdom here and now. Only then can we glimpse on earth the glory that awaits us in eternity.

HOW SHOULD WE RELATE TO WORLDLY GOODS?

As these saints demonstrate by their lives, the poor of spirit make the right choice: to enter heaven by the straight road and the narrow gate (Mt 7:13-14). What is here today and gone tomorrow cannot be given priority in the Christian life. Nothing is absolute but Almighty God. Thus, in Clare's words, we are to make "a great laudable exchange: to leave the things of time for those of eternity."[5]

The word "leave" must be rightly understood. It does not mean to cut ourselves off from those we love, or to forsake the goods we own as if they had no worth. Francis and Clare lived in radical and communal poverty, but they still made use of things—food, clothing, and shelter—to meet their needs and those of their brothers and sisters in Christ.

What is to be left behind are not God's gifts to us but our *inordi-*

nate attachment to these goods. As long as God comes first in our lives, we can love ourselves and all people and possessions as gifts to treasure, not objects to own and discard. We grow in Christian maturity when we learn to celebrate the gifts of God, but never to forget their giver. We can then depend on divine providence to care for our needs, while at the same time doing what we can to be good stewards of these gifts.

It is not possible to live this way without the dynamic of the "laudable exchange" of which Clare speaks:

- We exchange outer displays of detachment (such as giving up candy for Lent) for inner detachment (such as giving up our need to be the center of attention).

- We exchange our secret desires for wealth, status, and success for the willingness to accept obedience, chaste love, and poverty of spirit. God wants to give us these lasting treasures over and above any temporal rewards he may choose to bestow.

- We exchange our fascination with power, pleasure, and possession for the peace and joy Christ grants those who are poor in spirit. These dispositions, above all others, are the signs that we are living in consonance with God's will for our lives.

These exchanges reflect and confirm the fact that we have been placed on this earth not as owners but as stewards, not as managers but as caretakers and co-formers with God of all that he created. Selfish gain never proves to be a source of true and lasting happiness. In the end possessiveness always entraps us more than it frees us.

Real joy comes from attending to those divine invitations, challenges, and appeals to be generous with God's gifts to us. He wants us to share not only material goods but even more the gifts of teaching, preaching, counseling, parenting, befriending, aesthetic creation, and caring. Of what use is it to hoard what we have been given through no merit of our own?

TIME TO REFLECT

Allow this classical teaching from Scripture and the spiritual masters to encourage you in giving high priority to poverty of spirit. Growing in this virtue will lead you to the kingdom promised by your heavenly Father—the grace-filled place where divine guidance reigns, where holy wisdom outshines any amount of human knowledge. The following practical directives will help to point the way.

1. Rather than deny your limits, see them as unique chances to rely on God's providence every step of the way.

2. Instead of basing your well-being on worldly acclaim and vain notoriety, on your own projects and opinions, be quick to spot these weeds of pride and uproot them before they ruin the good fruit of humility. This practice takes vigilance.

3. Whether you are living in want or abundance, share what you have with others. Never endow possessions or prestige with any lasting worth. All these things pass away. What lasts is the law of God (Mt 5:17-19).

4. Try to look beyond people's surface needs to their inner wants. Be aware that God places them on your path for the sake of helping you to exercise poverty of spirit and generosity of heart.

5. Joyfully relinquish whatever prevents you from making Christ the center of your life so that you may more freely serve God's reign on earth. Remind yourself that you will receive a hundredfold in return.

6. Wait in peaceful surrender for any invitation from the Lord to give to others the goods you possess. Be glad for even the smallest opportunity to meet the material and spiritual needs of the poor.

7. Pay attention to inner stirrings prompting you to live a simpler lifestyle. Let the lives of St. Francis and St. Clare call you on in this effort.

8. Let go of extraneous goods that clutter your inner and outer house and crowd God out. You will find that traveling with less baggage is much more enjoyable in the long run. You are also likely to reach your goal of union with God more quickly.

9. Become more aware of the illusion of self-sufficiency. Realize how it prevents you from allowing the Holy Spirit to be the main guide of your life.

10. Pray for the gift of humility that makes you rejoice when others receive their due, while embracing your own destiny in the Lord. Be mindful of the snares of envy and jealousy that prevent you from celebrating the unique fullness of your own limited life call as well as that of others.[6]

SERVING YOU IN POVERTY OF SPIRIT
Adrian van Kaam

Dignity you bestowed abundantly
On every human being.
Each one is a sanctuary
Hiding the mystery of a mission
That outshines in the eyes of angels
Mundane appearance and success.

It may be a retarded child,
A sick old woman, an outcast of society,
A foreigner who talks haltingly,
Each one is splendid as a lustrous opal,
Precious as gold in the sight of God.

Each one is redeemed by the blood of Jesus
And called by the Spirit
To play a role in the kingdom
As will be known hereafter
When veils fall away
And the mystery of each life
Will stand revealed.

May I sing to people
About the mystery they deeply are,
About the Spirit in their plodding lives.
Already the fields are white
Ready for the harvest
But few are the laborers
To gather your chosen ones
Into the granary of the Spirit,
To separate the golden grain
Of their graced destiny
From the straw of attachment.

Lord, send me out into the fields.
And when I have done all I could,
Remind me kindly that I was only
A useless servant,
Serving you in poverty of spirit,
A humble mirror of my self-emptying Lord.

CHAPTER ELEVEN

Purity Opens Our Eyes of Faith

Blessed are the pure in heart; they shall see God.   **Matthew 5:8**

The tenth guideline to being guided by the Spirit of the Lord is this: *Be a single-hearted lover of God.*

Purity of heart calls for all of the preceding "be-attitudes." The marks of a God-guided life are repentance, conversion, forgiveness, compassion, docility, peacemaking, and poverty of spirit. The pure in heart concentrate their efforts on the one thing necessary in life, that which is above and beyond any other. Simply phrased, it is that God's will be done. This is the spring from whence Christian life flows, the vibrant source of our decisions and actions.

Mother Teresa of Calcutta exemplifies such purity of heart. When she looks into the eyes of the poor dying in her arms, she gazes into the eyes of Christ. She seems to find evidence of divine guidance everywhere, because she looks with eyes of love.

The woman who cleans our offices so well operates under the influence of the same spirit. Once we asked her how she remains so cheerful and lighthearted in the face of such a repetitious weekly task. Her answer struck us as simple yet profound:

"Because I love what I do, because I do it with Jesus at my side, because I want you people to be pleased." We appreciate this talented woman who makes pure spiritual devotion seem attainable for us as well.

When our hearts are undivided, we begin to see Christ revealed not only in our own lives but in the people and circumstances that comprise our field of vision. As we seek to live in the pure light of God's loving guidance, others begin to see us as mirrors of the divine mystery, as compassionate and peaceful people.

THE PROCESS OF PURIFICATION

As we discussed in the chapter on conversion, our hearts are not purified all at once. Transformation in Christ takes time. Whatever stands between us and God has to be removed, a cleansing process that entails considerable detachment. To use a nautical metaphor, the barnacles of the world have become firmly affixed to our hearts. One single scrape won't do the job.

We once met a chaplain in the United States Navy who described how this lesson had been driven home in his own life. This man prided himself on his ability to function well under any set of circumstances. He was conscious of attaining an excellent fitness report and of being in line for promotion. Having been assigned to a new base, the chaplain wanted to do everything he could to impress his commanding officer. So he was the first to report in the morning and the last to leave in the evening. He was a busy person, and the stack of papers on his desk proved it.

Early one day a knock came on his door. To the chaplain's surprise, it was his commanding officer.

"Chaplain," the C.O. said, "I'd like a word with you. Actually, I'd like to ask you a question."

"Of course, Sir, fire away."

"Maybe I'm not saying this properly, but where is it you people go when you need to remember what it is that you people are called to do?"

The chaplain was "knocked off his socks," as he said. The C.O. hinted at the word "retreat," and ordered this "man of God" to make one over the next three days. He added that what he needed on this base was not just a "military" chaplain but a "chaplain" who happened to be in the military.

Our chastened chaplain promptly booked a place in a nearby retreat house. When he got back to his quarters, he packed two bags. Into one he put his personal items such as pajamas and a shaving kit; into the other he swept the ten books he had on a chair next to his desk—the books he'd promised himself to read "when he had the time."

The moment of purgation, with the detachment it requires, occurred when the chaplain arrived at his mountaintop hideaway. He opened the trunk of his car, saw the two bags lying side by side, and suddenly realized what his C.O. was trying to tell him. In a deliberate act of surrender to God, the chaplain picked up the duffel bag with his overnight things and slammed the trunk shut with the books inside. For the next three days he spent time with God, more than he had since he entered the Navy. He saw with a purer heart the meaning of his call—to serve others as a minister of the Lord and not mainly as a military officer.

If *detachment* is the first step in the process of purgation, then *growth in humility* is the second. Humility enables us to be present to God just as we are, without all the props suggested by pride. Pride kills our receptivity to messages from our Divine Guide. Humility refines our capacity to listen and makes our hearts receptive to the graces infused by the Holy Spirit as illuminative gifts of God.

Pride almost prevented our chaplain friend from taking his commanding officer's invitation seriously. He bristled inwardly at the suggestion of a retreat, wondering just who his superior thought he was. Had he not caught himself in time, the chaplain would have been inclined to disobey these orders and break his own perfect record. Instead he swallowed his pride and listened humbly to the command to "go wherever it is that you people go when you need to remember what it is that you people are called to do."

Once on retreat, he felt grateful to his superior officer for bringing him to his knees. The chaplain had to admit that his prayer life was dry as dust. Our friend placed his divided heart before God for healing. After two days of inner stilling and spiritual reading, the light of insight dawned: "This was where God wanted me to be. I was his servant. He had chosen me to preach his Word. Whether I had extra stripes on my shirt or not, I was still a valuable instrument in his hands."

Detachment and humility allowed this man to see some dispositions of the heart—pride being the worst of them—that stood in the way of the next step in the process of purgation. This is God's highest gift to us, the step spiritual masters call *transforming union*. The chaplain tasted something of this longed-for nearness to God toward the end of his retreat.

He was able to get in touch with some of the obstacles to attaining what his retreat master called "contemplative union with the Trinity." One definite culprit was his bent toward being a functionary, if not a full-blown workaholic. The chaplain became convinced that he had to follow a different rhythm, to make more room in his day for person-to-Person meetings with the Lord. He had to preach Christ by living in union with him.

The chaplain prayed humbly and earnestly that grace would melt anything in his life that stood in the way of deeper at-oneness with the Divine. He wanted to be pure of heart. He prayed that the love of God would suffuse his whole being and spill over into his daily ministry. Maybe this is what his C.O. wanted after all. He hoped that he could at least return to the base having advanced a few steps on his journey to God.

We seek the same goal: to let ourselves be guided by a sacred purpose. We want to allow the life and love of the Trinity to flow through us, to behold the world as God's house where we serve his people with love. Only the pure in heart can see God in the faces of the people they meet.

Jesus was moved to compassion by human suffering (Mt 9:36;

14:14). Are we? Do we obey Christ's command to love the Lord
God with our whole heart (Mk 12:30)? Above all, are we beginning
to glorify God with one heart and one voice (Rm 15:6), with a song
that springs from a pure heart (1 Tm 1:5)?

FRUITS OF SINGLE-HEARTED LOVE

The barnacles of selfish concerns must be scraped from our
hearts by the purifying power of self-giving love. Purity of heart
protects us from becoming inwardly divided. It makes us sensitive
to any coercion or addiction that threatens to tear us away from the
transforming guidance of God. The same can be said of lesser
attachments. Otherwise they, too, would deflate our pledge to pursue God with single-hearted love.

We become more adept at dealing with the dissonance that dis-
turbs our ability to be present to the Lord in prayer. Distractions
lessen. Discouragement, discontent, depression, depletion, and
despair begin to give way when we consistently abandon ourselves
to the mystery of divine guidance. Courage and hope carry us
through trying times. Repletion and joy trail after us. And people
never fail to respond when we learn to "love one another intensely
from a [pure] heart" (1 Pt 1:22).

How easy it would be to lose ourselves in the lusts of life, to be
scattered in a thousand directions, to be so overextended we don't
have time to stand still and listen to God's guidance. Jesus describes
the fruit of an unclean heart in Matthew 15:9. He teaches us that
evil thoughts, murder, adultery, fornication, theft, false witness,
blasphemy—and all else that defile us—come from the heart. All
movements for or against God touch the heart. That is why inner
purity can abide in us only when our hearts have been reformed and
transformed by grace.

When we are preoccupied with ourselves, our vision narrows.
The pursuit of excessive ambitions exacts the price of restless dissi-
pation. We seem unable to perceive any order or pattern behind

events. They strike us as disconnected, as devoid of any providential design. We can feel as if we have been left on our own in the midst of an uncaring universe.

Purity of heart enables us to resist such a faithless view. We trust that behind what appears to be chaos there is a creative order guided by God. At privileged moments we sense in awe that beneath and beyond all diversity there lies a hidden unity, that behind the many there is the unspeakable One. Deep down we know that seeming disintegration conceals a mystery of divine integration, a personally loving force that guides the unfolding of the universe and our individual lives within it.

When we view life from this deeper dimension, our sense of direction improves. We live less in the illusion of exalted, autonomous control and more in the awareness of being servants of a benevolent and personal God. This seeing with the eyes of faith may not provide instant solutions to our problems, but it does help us to trust in the ultimate meaningfulness of whatever transpires on our formation journey.

Purity of heart fosters greater clarity of vision. We become able to view life and the world against the infinite vista of the Transcendent. We abandon our attempts to short-circuit this process through pseudo-spiritual "highs" or popularized expressions of spirituality.

We become convinced that our longing to see God cannot be satisfied by any kind of magic. What matters is our receptivity to his grace. Grace alone can make us realize how the simple events of everydayness are linked with the Father's loving will for our lives. Becoming aware of this connection is the goal of daily spiritual self-direction under the guidance of the Holy Spirit.

Seeing with the eyes of faith means celebrating the Transcendent in the here and now. It means detecting possibilities where others see only problems. To see as a single-hearted lover of God means waiting upon "what is" rather than filtering every event through the narrow grid of our own expectations of what should or ought to be.

A NEW WAY OF LOOKING AND LOVING

A Russian psychiatrist, who came to our Epiphany Center during his sabbatical, gave a farewell address to his American colleagues before his return to Moscow. His story provided an apt description of single-hearted seeing. This man is a specialist with two degrees, one in medicine and another in theology. Because he had to support his family during his studies here, he ended up working for about five months as a busboy in one of the finest restaurants in Pittsburgh. He couldn't help but wonder, *What is the meaning of my doing this? What is God's will for me?*

The answer began to emerge as he tried to appraise his situation in the light of what he had learned about spiritual formation. "My lack of money became an invitation to foster contacts with people I would otherwise not have met. I grew in the conviction that to mature spiritually I had to accept the challenge to leave my comfortable study room and go to work."

Once he started his job, he could easily see the positive side of being a busboy. In fact, he described it as an "unforgettable event, a highlight of my American experience." In accordance with the call of divine guidance, he was able to grow in what he refers to as a "waiter's spirituality."

This psychiatrist saw that the primary aim of a waiter is to be a *servant*. He reflected upon the Greek word *therapon*, from which we derive both the English words "physician" and "therapist." This word originally meant a trained, honest, attentive, obedient, and responsible *servant*. He perceived that God's will for him while he was in this country included learning how to be a better servant.

He first focused on the attitude of detachment. He explained how he experienced this:

The atmosphere of a good restaurant is that of a feast. People come here to celebrate the important events of their lives, holidays, anniversaries, birthdays, or simply to show that they are in a good mood. They want to spend time enjoying tasteful food and music. They prepare themselves for this event by wearing beautiful dresses and using fine perfumes.

The crucial point of service is the awareness on the part of the waiter that he is not a participant in the customer's joy, but only a facilitator. He must detach himself from the provocative smells of delicious food, from the sometimes seductive clothing of the customers, from the interesting conversations at table. To maintain his own integrity, he must keep inner spiritual purity by practicing a vigilant kind of detachment. This formative attitude can preserve him from envy, empty curiosity, and greed.

Our Russian friend went on to talk about another positive aspect of a waiter's spirituality: cultivating an interest in the act of serving itself. "I remember what a fellow worker once said to me: 'Just imagine that your relatives are sitting here and you want to please them.' In other words, this is the moment of unconditional appreciation."

Our friend became a busboy out of economic necessity; this humble job led him to praise God. Far from feeling abandoned by the power of divine guidance, this man allowed hints of transcendence to redeem what might have been for someone else a demeaning, financially hopeless situation. He found a new reason for offering service. He became sensitive to his own and others' unvoiced needs, wishes, thoughts, and feelings. He tried to respond to each situation with the finesse it deserved rather than reacting to it resentfully or thoughtlessly. And, by the grace of God, we are sure he returned to Moscow with greater purity of heart.

Have we cleansed our hearts of selfish tendencies? Do we welcome Jesus and others in a companionship of love and appreciation? If we can answer yes to both questions, then it is safe to say we are on the way to living in the pure light of God's loving guidance.

WHAT DOES IT MEAN TO SEE GOD?

To see God with purity of heart is a grace we cannot command. To cooperate with this grace, we must be willing to remove whatever blocks our vision of God. In this context, the *heart* signifies the whole person. Consequently, purity of heart expresses our readiness to let God's love suffuse our entire being, to allow his will to direct our lives from beginning to end.

Purification is painful. It can feel like a refining fire (Mal 3:2). Yet the effect of this graced event is the blessing of seeing God in a way that makes us forget the pain of the process. This new vision enhances and nourishes purity of heart. "Everyone who has this hope [of seeing God as he is]... makes himself pure, as [God] is pure" (1 Jn 3:3).

This purification of heart is not a once-and-for-all process. It happens in stages over an extended period of time. The fire of our love for God gradually burns away all lesser loves or attachments. Anytime we bind ourselves in an exclusive way to little "gods" of our own making, we feel hampered and restrained. These lesser loves cause our hearts to drift away from the One who alone can fulfill us.

Like an early warning system, pangs of conscience prompt us to detach ourselves from self-centered tendencies. Contrition frees us to love God for his own sake, not merely for the gifts he grants us. Purging the heart of unworthy attachments is complemented by a longing to be open to disclosures and directives of the Holy Spirit in whatever persons, events, and things come our way.[1] Purity of heart does not destroy excessive attachments. It reforms them and absorbs them into the love of God.

Purity of heart involves humble affirmation of our creatureliness, together with the hope that God will draw us into deeper intimacy with the Trinity. Such participation is impossible to attain unless, with the help of grace, our hearts break free from what is impure and become pliable to the touch of God. The heart of stone will not be able to see God's presence in daily life. We are free to accept or to refuse the surrender that may flower into new "showings" of God's presence.

Despite our sinfulness, God wants us to become members of the Triune family by adoption. Our *Abba*—"Father"—has seen and accepted us from the start. Even in our disobedience, God did not cease loving us. So great is his affection for us that he reached into human history to heal the rift between himself and us due to Adam's sin (Rom 5:12-17). He gave us his Word, his only Son, as the bridge to our salvation. Jesus blesses the pure in heart because they manifest in both their attitudes and actions the spiritual fruits of joy, patience, mercy, gentleness, peace, trustworthiness, and self-control (Gal 5:13-26).

When we have made progress by no longer yielding to self-indulgence, we can better put on the Lord Jesus Christ (Rom 13:14). We can live Christ-centered lives. In the common routines of home or business, in the drabness of passing days, in moments of joy or sorrow, we can strive to see the Lord as we are seen by him. This divinized seeing is the Lord's gift to us. Through it, he embraces the whole world and each unique person in it.

Through the power of the Holy Spirit, forms of impurity such as indecency, idolatry, and cruelty can cease to exist amid the children of light. The effects of this light are seen in increased goodness, right living, and truth (Eph 5:1-14). The love of God enables God's friends to give up everything that does not lead to him. His grace so purifies their hearts that they have no other ambition than to do what he asks (Ti 2:11-15).

Only when our hearts are freed from the impurity of pride and self-indulgence can we enjoy the gift of contemplative seeing. The pure heart is the focal point of contemplative transformation. It is like a compass that helps us to find our way through thickets of confusion and misdirection. As we follow the pathway revealed to the pure heart by divine guidance, our whole life becomes a more perfect mirror of the life of Jesus.

Many attitudes may prepare us for this transformation, but only the redemptive love of Jesus can keep us rightly motivated. Thus freed from worldly attachments, we can love God with our whole being and others in him. In short, we begin to rest in the shadow of what we shall see fully in the life to come. Here human reason fails and faith ascends. Mind begins to flow into heart. We begin to fix our gaze adoringly on God in loving contemplation, glorifying him with one heart and one voice (Rom 15:6) now and for all ages to come.

In the words of St. John of the Cross (1542-1591), "Cleanness of heart is nothing less than the love and grace of God. The pure of heart are called blessed by our Savior [Mt 5:8], and to call them blessed is equivalent to saying they are taken with love, for blessedness is derived from nothing else but love."[2]

TIME TO REFLECT

The goal of a faith-filled, God-guided life is to break through the illusory loves of an unpurged heart, to become pliable to the touch of God, to finally *see* God. To help you move from a scattered existence to a life centered in Christ, we offer the following counsels.

1. Cultivate an habitual desire to imitate Christ in all that you are and do. Seek to bring your life into conformity with his. If he were standing by your side, what would you say or do?

2. Candidly acknowledge emotional distractions and devious ambitions that diminish your single-minded adherence to divine guidance. Ask for the grace to turn away from them.

3. Try not to scatter your attention and affection in numerous, superfluous directions that fragment your quest for purity of heart and purpose of life.

4. Be careful not to emphasize *being busy* to the exclusion of simply *being*. Do not engage in work so intensely that awe for the divine mystery dies and your inner life becomes more disparaging than appreciative.

5. Take time to wait upon any disclosure of the secret leadings of the Lord in the routine activities of your day.

6. Cultivate heartfelt confidence in the Spirit's guiding of your life, no matter how obscure or hidden this direction may be.

7. Courageously take the risk of giving up ultimate control over your life and the false sense of security it brings.

8. Temper reasoning by faith. Try to let go of images or ideas that tend to reduce God to your level and learn to worship the Lord in spirit and in truth (Jn 4:23).

9. In all that you are and do, proceed from an undivided heart to seek the glory of God and the good of others. Be prepared to endure pain and persecution. Decide not to be deterred from your quest.

10. Be ready to behold manifestations of the Most High in the most unexpected places. Release your grip on life and give yourself over to the God who surprises.

PURITY OF HEART
Adrian van Kaam

Mystery of Eternal Love,
Grant me purity of heart,
Free my heart from arrogance,
From goals too sublime for me.

Still and quiet my excited heart
As a mother quiets the little one on her lap.
Still my unclean drive for mere achievement.
Make my heart less divided,
More peaceful and pure in intent.

Let the warmth of your loving heart
Melt my calculating, cold ambitions.

Mystery of Eternal Love,
Make my heart a clean channel
For the outflow of your warmth
In this icy world where hearts are frozen.

Your heart embraces universe, humanity, and history;
Embrace my lonely heart,
Free it from fear and calculation,
Make me sense the wonder of salvation.

CHAPTER TWELVE

Responding to the Grace of Guidance

Abba, Father!... Take this cup away
from me. But let it be as you, not I,
would have it.   **Mark 14:36**

The eleventh practical guideline to God's guidance can be summed up in two words: *Listen and respond.*

Zechariah refused to listen to the angel's good news from God: Elizabeth would bear a son destined to prepare the way of the Lord. Because of his lack of trust, he was struck mute until the day of circumcision. When he responded by naming the baby John, Zechariah was filled with the Holy Spirit and broke into a glorious song of praise.

We find a clue to the all-transcending mystery of divine guidance in Zechariah's Canticle as prayed in the Liturgy of the Hours: "In the tender compassion of our God, the dawn from on high shall break upon us, to shine on those who dwell in darkness and the shadow of death, and to guide our feet into the way of peace" (cf. Lk 1:78-79).

God shows his love for us by shining his holy light into our darkened hearts. These intimations of divine direction do not come to us like lightning bolts from the sky or fiery lava from a volcano. Rather, Zechariah compares these tender signs of God's compassion to the "dawn from on high."

Dawn appears slowly on the horizon. It does not rush to reveal at once the brightness of the day. The light of dawn comes to us in soft hues that fill us with wonder. *Have you not been touched on an early morn by the fragile lacework-quilt of dew strung from leaves and flowers? How many times have you missed these graced in-breaking moments?* Often we are too busy to notice the gift of the dawn, too preoccupied to attend to divine disclosures in the midst of everydayness.

A friend of ours named Joyce shared her experience of becoming aware of God's inspiration. These divine movements were at first too delicate for her to recognize, but as time passed she began to realize the guiding lights they carried for her life. Her eyes were opened to the dawning, especially at her lowest ebbs of disappointment.

After the sheer accumulation of several small enlightenments had broken in upon her, Joyce began to see what God had intended for her from the start. From that moment until now, our friend has never ceased to marvel at the way God is directing her life. She has to be still and listen, but she knows that divine guidance will come.

"At times," Joyce says, "I feel like a dry, dusty field that has been drenched by a fresh, spring rain, so sure am I of God's love for me. At other times I sense only blistering, cloudless days looming over the horizon. Dry spells deplete my strength once again, but I know I am not alone. I offer God my good intentions. I do my spiritual exercises. These fluctuations of light and shadow do not surprise or paralyze me anymore. I accept consolation and desolation, certitude and uncertainty, as messengers of the divine, proclaiming the guidance I need at this moment of my life."

Joyce learned from personal experience that divine guidance is a gift of transforming love. God led her step-by-step to where he wanted her to go: into the promised land of likeness to his holy will. As we go, and usually when we least expect it, "the dawn from on high shall break upon us," and we shall be more ready than ever to follow the Lord toward a new day.

THE GIFT OF OBEDIENCE

As the mysterious workings of grace arouse our awe and our appreciation, the best response we can give is a listening heart. *Discovering* God's will goes hand in hand with *obeying* whatever guidance we receive. One is a call, the other a response. Both significantly influence the present direction of our lives and the shape they will take in the future.

In all that happens to you, God wants to draw you closer to himself. But he cannot do so alone. He needs your cooperation.

The kernel of our cooperation with God's guidance is *obedience*, but we can be obedient to the Spirit's voice only if we can first hear its soft whisper. Often we cannot hear that shy sound of the Mystery. Why not? Because our heart is like that of Martha's when Jesus visited with her and her sister, Mary (Lk 10:38-42).

Jesus gently reproached Martha because she was busy with many things, whereas only one thing was necessary. He did not chide her for taking care of the house and the meal. Good housekeeping is one of the works of loving service inspired by God. What Jesus reproached was the fact that Martha allowed this labor to make her so anxious and restless that she could no longer hear the voice of the Spirit within her heart. She had lost touch with her call to obedient openness.

We should serve, of course, but our service should be animated by divine love, however busy we may be. To keep in touch with the voice of the Holy Spirit in our hearts, we must maintain inner stillness even in the midst of our daily labors. We must listen to Christ's invitation, "Follow me" (Jn 1:43).

Whenever we hear his call, we cannot of ourselves instantly obey. *Obedience is a grace, a gift of the Holy Spirit.* It will be given to us only if we long for it and deepen our longing day by day. We must not only desire the grace of obedience but pray for it continuously. Then in God's own time, we may be granted moments of stillness that tame the restlessness of our hearts. Gradually these moments may last longer. As time passes, they may become interconnected.

In the end, they, too, may become almost continuous.

Our peace of heart is assailed by many of the distractions Jesus admonished in Martha. We are taken out of any semblance of a contemplative stance by our tendency to socialize, by countless telephone conversations, by a cacophony of voices coming from newspapers, billboards, supermarkets, advertisements, commercials, and current events. The noise never seems to stop.

If we are not careful, our restless hearts become filled with idle longings, like a wilderness of weeds that overtakes the tender flower of God's guidance and our call to obey his gentle leading. We must beg the Spirit to bring order into the chaos of our overstimulated hearts. That is the beginning of enlightened obedience, a necessary prelude to the fullness of obedience we all seek.

The song of an obedient heart is like a soft melody of steady surrender of desires that are at odds with divine guidance. Because of sin, we often sing out of tune. Like a loving director, our Father in heaven sent his eternal Word to help us play the music of eternity. Jesus took up our simple and painful human existence and shows us, despite sin, how to live in obedient surrender.

We need to meditate on the mysteries of Christ's life as told to us in the Gospels, to make our home in the events that marked the stages of his surrender to the Father's will. The more we do so, the more we shall be able to lift our daily lives—with all their unruly notes of discordant and disobedient thoughts and deeds—and sing in tune with the risen Christ. Then divine light will clarify the secret places in our lives where surrender is still lacking.

Jesus himself will go with us to guide our journey. He will show us how to let the Spirit lead us step-by-step. Waves of adversity may drench us, winds of temptations may almost sweep us away from our chosen path. People may betray and undermine us, whether in outright treachery or merely ignorant disregard. We may die countless daily deaths. But as long as we unite our crosses and our dyings with the cross and death of Christ, we shall live with the risen Lord until the day of glory dawns.

THE TOUCH OF GRACE

Jesus cried out in the garden of Gethsemane, "*Abba*, Father!... Take this cup away from me. But let it be as you, not I, would have it" (Mk 14:36). He invites us to enter our own individual gardens of agony along the way to holiness. Once we hear his invitation, we need to pray for the grace to follow him.

Even though we may want to live in obedience to the will of the Father, saying yes to suffering never comes easily. It is grace that lifts us beyond our fear of failure, our lack of vision, our longing for felt consolations rather than for the God who consoles. Grace makes us see that we can remain joy-filled while bearing the cross.

Holy Scripture and the writings of the spiritual masters guide us in the dark and uncertain moments of daily life. As Paul says in his letter to the Romans, all depends on faith; all is a grace; we are to "[hope] against hope" (Rom 4:16-18).

Grace, as Paul tells us, is about the "how much more" of God's love for us. It is about the unmerited gift of divine redemption. He writes, "The gift is not like the transgression. For if by that one person's transgression the many died, *how much more* did the grace of God and the gracious gift of the one person, Jesus Christ, overflow for the many" (Rom 5:15).

Paul's text makes clear that divine grace transforms and deepens all our gifts. He reminds us that "thanks" is too small a word for this miracle of grace that transcends yet lovingly embraces, elevates, and penetrates our lives: "Everything indeed is for you, so that the grace bestowed in abundance on more and more people may cause the thanksgiving to overflow for the glory of God" (2 Cor 4:15).

A chaplain once told the story of a soldier who had hesitantly approached him before he went into battle in Vietnam. His mother had sent this young man a rosary, and he wanted to have it blessed by a Catholic priest. As it turned out, the army chaplain was a Southern Baptist! But they were in the middle of a war. So, as kindly as he could, the chaplain took the soldier aside, covered the hand that held the beads, and together they said the Lord's Prayer and asked for God's protection.

The young man was satisfied. He felt sure that he had fulfilled his mother's request as best he could under the circumstances. Several weeks later, this Baptist minister was visiting the field hospital to console the wounded. He began speaking to a soldier who looked slightly familiar. It was the man whose rosary he had blessed.

Seeing him lying on a cot in obvious misery, the chaplain apologized profusely, "I guess I didn't give you a good enough blessing, son." The soldier smiled warmly and assured him that he had done more than he realized for him. He had been shot, but with his blessed rosary around his neck, he was still alive. "And, chaplain, thanks to the grace of God, I'm going home! I'd like to give you my rosary before I leave."

When we were told this touching story, the chaplain chuckled and said, "I don't know how many Southern Baptist pastors have rosary beads, but I treasure mine."

The grace of divine guidance is a sign of the goodness of the Trinity that knows no bounds.[1] It goes beyond gifts of nature such as bodily health, the sharpness of a sound mind, the comfort of good food, a warm coat on a cold day, or a roof over our heads when it rains. Grace may use anything to help us to grow—from a blessed rosary on a battlefield, to a striking scene in nature, to the stranger we meet on the street. All can be windows opened by grace to remind us of God's gentle love and care.

Both the soldier and the army chaplain saw how divine guidance embraces our lives as a whole. And both of them were grateful to their gracious God. After relating this tale in one of his services, the chaplain prayed: "Almighty and ever faithful God, source of all that is good, from the beginning of time you promised us that you will help us to be always faithful. Give us the grace we need to serve you with joy, and to know forever the peace of your presence. Help us to live lives of constant service to those in need. This we ask in the name of Jesus our Savior."

ACCEPTING THE PACE OF GRACE

The wonder and mystery of divine guidance is such that we can never achieve, demand, or control it. The origin of the word "grace" helps us to appreciate its marvels: it comes from the Greek *charis*, meaning the benevolence shown by the "gods" to the human race. The grace of divine guidance is God's greatest gift. It is the indispensable means enabling us to abandon the illusion of self-reliance and to cling to the providence of God. No human effort can attain divine grace. It is a gift that enlightens our faith journey, even in the darkest hour.

To receive and respond to this gift, we must first acknowledge, at least implicitly, that our lives cannot be transformed without the guiding light and gratuitous assistance of a power greater than ourselves or any collection of human experts.

However astute our study or practice of spiritual direction may be, divine grace alone can give us the insight and the courage we need to turn our wills and our lives over to our Beloved. We can do so with shouts of joy, as did the first Christians at Pentecost, or more commonly with fear and trembling. Either response connects us to the amazing grace that led Paul to say: "Thanks be to God for his indescribable gift!" (2 Cor 9:15).

This mysterious gift of grace can transform rebellious, confused, and cowardly people into stalwart pillars of Christ-centered living. Paul himself is an example of the difference divine guidance can make. He clearly states and demonstrates by his life what discipleship demands and what it offers. It calls for obedience to legitimate authority, but it also prevents us from being "carried away by all kinds of strange teaching." Thus it is good, as Paul says, "to have our hearts strengthened by grace" (Heb 13:9).

At crossroad moments in our journey, when God wants to guide us through a crisis, we may need to seek the help of a wise and experienced spiritual guide. He or she may be the channel grace uses to help us to flow again into the blessed sea of prayerful presence and action.

Sooner or later we will discover that there is never enough security, power, and success to fill the void in our hearts. Sometimes it feels as if we are floundering outside the will of God like a fish floundering on the shore. Human achievements such as graduating from college, finding a job, or raising a family can contribute significantly to our sense of personal dignity and worth, but more is needed to make us truly happy.

We may enjoy passing moments, even long periods of satisfaction, but there comes a time when only a deeper relationship with God will do. To avoid the temptations of either apathy or abdication of responsibility, we may need to find a spiritual director, friend, or counselor to help us. If such a person is not readily available, we can always turn to spiritual reading for guidance.

One such guide whom we meet in the classical literature of Christian spirituality is the anonymous monk of fourteenth-century England mentioned in chapter four. His famous treatise on divine direction, *The Cloud of Unknowing*, encourages us to stop turning over in our minds the unanswerable questions. Once we do so, we may be ready to listen to the guiding whispers of God's call in the core of our being.

The author knows that we often find it hard to hear the shy sounds of divine disclosures. He encourages us by saying: "There is no one lacking this grace who has not the capacity to receive it, whether he be sinful or innocent. For the grace is not given because of innocence, nor is it withheld because of sin.... God gives it freely without any meriting."[2]

How then ought we to respond to the grace of divine guidance? This wise monk gives the following advice:

> Try to be the wood and let it [grace] be the carpenter; the house, and let it be the husbandman dwelling in the house.... It is enough for you that you feel moved in love by something, though you do not know what it is; so that in this affection you have no thought of anything in particular under God, and that your reaching out is simply directed to God.... Trust steadfastly

that it is God alone who moves your will and your desire; he alone, entirely of himself, without any intermediary.[3]

Once we have experienced the reshaping and redirecting grace of God and its guiding power, we must admit in humility that our quest for spiritual direction does not end there; it is only beginning. Like a butterfly that escapes the catcher's net, steadfast trust in divine providence often eludes us during the ups and downs of daily life. The moment things cease to go our way, the sour gases of distrust, fear, impatience, and disaffection bubble to the surface. We once again see life as threatening rather than as a tender disclosure of God's guiding grace.

The author of *The Cloud of Unknowing*, like all good spiritual directors, advises us to forget these debilitating fears and turn our faces back toward the sun of divine light. Instead of growing impatient because we have not become holy overnight, we need to become advent people and await God's coming once again. Patient endurance, not exhausting willfulness, wins the race of faith.

In God's good time, the grace of divine guidance will point us to the way of transformation. It will free us from anxious rumination and help us to appreciate God's will in our here-and-now situation. Divine grace will purify and enhance the limited gifts of self-direction we have been granted. It will make us more sensitive to the presence of God in the people, events, and things around us.

Such guidance mellows any harsh, perfectionist attempts to whip ourselves into shape. The Spirit of wise counsel reminds us to let go of the reins of control and to turn to God in our weakness. With the apostle Paul, we are not ashamed to say, "If I must boast, I will boast of the things that show my weakness" (2 Cor 11:30).

Whenever problems of life direction do arise, we ought not to feel compelled to solve them instantly. Divine guidance takes time. To push against the pace of grace may lead us to an illusory peace that will soon dissipate under pressure. What we seek is neither complacency nor stagnation; both are false forms of spirituality.

We must allow the grace of divine guidance to lead us when we are lost in the wilderness of our anxious, self-directed search for happiness and holiness. Though we sometimes cannot see the forest for the trees, we must trust that the Lord is taking us on a journey from clearing to clearing. When we are held down by the shackles of self-centeredness, we cannot enjoy the bracing air of the wide open spaces opened up for us by grace at appropriate times. We think we have to bear the burden of "going it alone," and once again get lost in the dense woods of endless, convoluted ruminations.

Even in these wilderness experiences, our Divine Guide has readied another clearing. With Christ at our side, we can weather every storm. Even in times of pain and overwhelming problems, we can find a way to thank God for the "dew of grace" that descends on those who humbly try to say yes.

The author of *The Cloud of Unknowing* aptly describes how we should respond during these difficult phases of our journey:

> It is the nature of stones to be dry and hard, and where they strike, there one feels it sorely. These physical exertions are very firmly fixed to the sensible feelings, and they are very dry, in that they lack the dew of grace…. So beware of these beast-like efforts, and learn to love with true fervor, with a gentle and peaceful disposition, both in body and soul. And wait patiently on the will of our Lord with courtesy and humility, and do not snatch at it hurriedly, like a greedy greyhound, no matter how hungry you may be.[4]

We can trust that at the end of the darkest tunnel the light will shine. We await the day when we shall be united with our Beloved for all eternity. If this means ascending to God through adversity, so be it. Nothing can deter us when the Holy Spirit is our guide. When the sky darkens, we can follow in faith the star of abandonment that pierces our night. We can listen to the music of eternity.[5] With Christ, we can say, "Father, into your hands I commend my spirit" (Lk 23:46).

TIME TO REFLECT

The following five questions will help you to avail yourself of the grace-filled openings granted to you by the Holy Spirit. You may answer these privately, or with a spiritual director, or with a group of like-minded Christians. We have suggested readings from Scripture and the spiritual masters, and noted the primary theme of each text in parentheses. Consult the bibliography for full references.

You will find this an effective way to break the bondage of self-centeredness, to listen and respond to the grace of divine guidance. As you allow yourself to be guided by the Director of directors, the Holy Spirit, you will begin to enjoy the steady companionship of your blessed Lord.

1. Have I in the course of my faith and formation journey thus far come to know Jesus Christ as my personal God and Savior?

    Scripture: Ephesians 1:3-4 ("He chose us"); John 15:16 ("It was not you who chose me").

    The Confessions of St. Augustine, p. 202 ("All the dark shadows of doubt fled away").

2. Have I been faithful to my unique-communal life call in the Lord? Have I kept the faith?

    Scripture: 1 John 2:24-29 (God's anointing teaches you about everything; remain in him); 2 Timothy 1:14 ("The Spirit dwells within us").

    The Way of Perfection by St. Teresa of Avila, p. 103 ("I never lost confidence in his mercy").

3. What is the composition of my daily devotional life and do I give it the highest priority?

    Scripture: Romans 12:9-21 ("Do not be conquered by evil but conquer evil with good"); 1 Thessalonians 5:16-18 ("Pray without ceasing").

Introduction to the Devout Life by St. Francis de Sales, pp. 43-44 ("Bring forth the fruits of devotion, each according to his or her position and vocation").

4. How diligent am I in maintaining this devotional life? What keeps me from growing discouraged when I feel dry?

   Scripture: Philippians 4:4-9 ("By prayer and petition, with thanksgiving, make your requests known to God"); 1 Timothy 4:13-15 (Be diligent in these matters, be absorbed in them).

   The Practice of the Presence of God by Brother Lawrence of the Resurrection, pp. 123-124 (God's continual presence is the most fruitful kind of prayer).

5. Is my heart open to the inspirations of the Holy Spirit? Do my decisions and actions flow from my understanding of discipleship?

   Scripture: 1 Peter 1:13-25 ("Be holy yourselves in every aspect of your conduct"); Romans 12:2 (Discern what is the will of God).

   The Imitation of Christ by Thomas à Kempis, p. 64 ("The kingdom of God is within you"; make room for Christ).

RESPONDING TO GRACE
Adrian van Kaam

Responding to grace,
Without hurry or haste,
Means dwelling in you who makes new my day,
Who lessens my fascination with futile ways,
Awakening me to what only remains.

Keep touching me inwardly
Until the light of insight dawns.
Do not allow the flicker of light to die
Before it becomes a living flame consuming me.
Make me treasure the dawn that speaks inaudibly.
Make me cherish the moment of illumination,
Attune me to the tender beginnings
Of grace-filled inspiration.

Thaw the tundra of my soul,
Uproot the weeds that choke your gift.
Till the soil, dig the furrows
In which your grace may softly sink
To weather the winter of my heart.

Do not allow your grace in me
To dwindle like seed
Choked off by weeds
That suffocate and drain its power.

Oasis in the wasteland of my life,
Still the noise of daily chatter
That I may hear anew the murmur
Of the living waters
Running through the universe.

Mellow me, refine my receptivity
That I may surrender graciously
To the blessings you bestow on me.
Let me hear your invitation whispered gently
Like the rains of spring.
Give me an angel's wing
To rise with you, Eternal Lord,
To light the shadows of this dying earth
With candles of compassion.

CHAPTER THIRTEEN

Fulfilling Our Call

I have fought the good fight, I have finished the race, I have kept the faith.

2 Timothy 4:7

The twelfth and final practical guideline to being guided by God is what enables us to find true happiness in this life: *Be faithful to your call.*

Holy Scripture underscores the importance of fidelity to the divine call throughout the course of salvation history. Consider how God guided Ruth toward a journey of discovery. This Moabite woman was free to accept or reject his appeal. She took a chance, saying to Naomi the words that changed her life: "Do not ask me to abandon or forsake you! For wherever you go I will go, wherever you lodge I will lodge, your people shall be my people, and your God my God" (Ru 1:16).

Having banished alien gods from her life, Ruth was able to find and fulfill her call. In his First Epistle to the Corinthians, Paul describes his own call as well as ours in these words: "To you who have been sanctified in Christ Jesus, called to be holy, with all those everywhere who call on the name of our Lord Jesus Christ, their Lord and ours. Grace to you and peace from God our Father and the Lord Jesus Christ" (1 Cor 1:2-3).

Our call to be a holy people entails a consecration of our lives in and with Christ to the Father. The bread of our daily responsibilities and the wine of our sufferings are transformed through the power of the Holy Spirit. He is the faithful counselor and guide who leads us to commit our lives fully and freely to God.

FAITHFUL WITNESSES

We all know of the work of Mother Teresa of Calcutta, who has dedicated her life to easing the plight of millions of poor and dying throughout the world. When asked how she could carry on with her mission with so little evidence of success, she is said to have replied, "I am not here to be successful but to be faithful."

Most of us view Mother Teresa as a huge success, not in worldly terms but in doing the work of God. Even those who don't profess Christianity respect this diminutive and humble woman from Bulgaria. Yet no matter how small a dent we ourselves make in remedying the ills of society or earning the admiration of others, we are here not to be successful but to be faithful to our call. If we view success according to this world's standards, we would never dare to proclaim: "Behold the cross on which hangs the salvation of the world!"

One woman we know felt she had a vocation to live a solitary life as a poet. She never intended to fall in love but she did. Having relinquished the joys of solitude, she discovered to her delight a vocation to marriage. At the time we met this faithful follower of God, her children were already grown. She was still writing poetry, but she had also chosen to enrich her later years with still another vocation, to full-time parish ministry.

Another man, a monk now in his seventies, is also the father of four children and grandfather of two. After his wife died, this man felt urged by God to enter a monastery. He had been praying the Divine Office for many years but was not convinced he had a monastic vocation. He deliberately delayed following this leading for seven years to be sure he was not merely escaping his responsibilities or seeking security.

This man of prayer actively sought God's will by making several retreats and visiting the monastery he thought he wanted to enter. He kept appraising his decision until he felt more certain it was led by God. Only then did he dare ask permission to enter the novitiate. Now a professed monk, this man is a living witness to the diverse ways divine guidance can take. He has been faithful to God's call in his life. Once a husband and a businessman, he is now a gardener, a guest master, and a grandfather!

In the everyday world of raising children, paying bills, keeping schedules, cooking, working, sleeping, praying, we easily lose sight of the undercurrent of divine guidance that carries us along. Yet it is in the anonymity of such common duties and cares that our divine call becomes illumined. Within the everyday world of family and parish life, of labor and leisure, we must strive to be as faithful as Jesus was in Nazareth.

WHAT ABOUT THE DETOURS ALONG THE WAY?

Even our best efforts to be faithful to our call are no guarantee that we will always take the right road. Detours are inevitable when we allow divine guidance to lead us into the unknown. After all, we are sinners in need of redemption. We do not always listen to divine inspiration. We easily miss God's leading because of sin or distraction. We often resist or even refuse to obey what we hear.

We need to remember that our heavenly Father graciously awaits the return of any prodigal son or daughter, even one who rejects or avoids the divine call (Lk 15:11-32). Repentance from disobedience is always possible. No life is irreversibly lost in the eyes of the Good Shepherd, who leaves the flock to go after the one lamb gone astray (Lk 15:4).

When we do lose our way, we ought not to worry. We can trust that God will get us back on track later when we are more willing and able to obey. Or he may lead us to an entirely new vocation, one that is more sanctifying for us at a particular time of our lives.

In due time, we will regain the path to obedience.

Whenever we feel lost along the way, we can also rely on the exemplary words and deeds of those who have gone before us, and those who are still near and dear to us. We can consult a guidebook like this one, or the many spiritual readings we have recommended, or an expert in the field of spiritual direction.[1] We are not meant to travel alone, but as part of the people of God.

Simply put, faithfulness does not mean never making a mistake. God expects us to fight the good fight to the end, to stay faithful to his Word and to his call in our hearts. Grace will guide us if we make a sincere effort to run the race to the finish. Faith in God's mercy and forgiveness will sustain us. When we fall, the Lord will help us to rise again. That is his promise, and we must not doubt it for a minute.

Fear and fascination commingle in our hearts in the light of each disclosure we receive. Yet faith assures us that God does not want our lives to be wasted. Even when we make a huge mistake or take a lengthy detour, Christ promises to forgive and heal us, to help us make a new start.

LEAPING INTO THE UNKNOWN

We inevitably experience in the course of trying to fulfill our call that we are searchers, pilgrims, sojourners on the road to we know not where. More often we feel like plumbers trying to fix a sudden leak in our spiritual pipes, or electricians trying to recircuit our divine receivers. Sometimes we may even feel like astronauts lost in the vastness of space, hurtling at astronomical speeds toward a horizon that is constantly receding.

Who among us has not been threatened—even terror-stricken at times—by the awareness that we do not know *where* God wants to lead us? What is not predictable cannot be controlled, no matter how much we try.

The human spirit is like a camera with a complex focusing mechanism. It usually takes time to bring the full picture clearly into view. We can never predict the exact way God would have us go, nor can we know in explicit detail the kind of guidance we will receive or how it will come. At times we know with surprising clarity what God wants. More often, however, we can catch only a tiny glimmer of a particular facet of our life direction.

God calls us at times to plunge into the unknown depths of his love, trusting that he will keep us from drowning. More often than not, we respond by gathering up all of our courage and dipping one foot into the cold water of uncertainty.

To trust God in this way is like taking a leap in the dark over a steep ravine. No wonder we hesitate before committing ourselves to a major step in life such as marrying or staying single, embracing the celibate life, becoming a priest or minister, joining a religious community, or developing another outlet for our Christian presence. Such basic decisions are never easy to make. That is why we need the help of wise guides and good books.

The same feeling of hesitation may arise when we respond to our call in less momentous matters. We may want to flee from the duties imposed on us by daily life. We may try to escape to some imaginary place of easy obligations and pleasant companions. We miss the point that what God asks of us has to be faced here and now. We cannot reap the future rewards of being faithful unless we are willing to address the mundane demands of the present.

Whether the decision is momentous or mundane, whether we forge ahead in what may be foolhardy boldness or tiptoe forward in wise trepidation, God promises to go with us. Faith assures us, despite every uncertainty, that our Divine Caller will not leave us alone and forsaken. In the Last Supper discourse, Jesus assures us: "I will not leave you orphans; I will come to you. In a little while the world will no longer see me, but you will see me, because I live and you will live" (Jn 14:18-19).[2]

UNFORESEEN OUTCOMES OF FIDELITY

In a classical text that many view as a little bible of divine guidance, *The Imitation of Christ*, Thomas à Kempis (d. 1471) gives us this piece of sound advice about living in the epiphany of the present moment: "Every day we should renew our resolve to live a holy life, and every day we should kindle ourselves to a burning love, just as if today were the first day of our new life in Christ. We should say: 'Help me, Lord God, to fulfill my good intention and your holy service. Starting today, let me begin perfectly, for what I have done so far is nothing.'"[3]

This masterful text reminds us of the saying of Jesus: "When you have done all you have been commanded, say, 'We are unprofitable servants; we have done what we were obliged to do'" (Lk 17:10). Every event in life, from the birth of a child to the death of a parent, occurs within the providential love of God. Every encounter, from a passing meeting with a friend to the exchange of marriage vows, shapes and forms our sense of meaning and purpose. Every experience, from dressing for work in the morning to cooking in the evening, provides an opportunity to glorify God by the work of human hands.

What transpires in the course of fulfilling our call remains a mystery known fully only to the Trinity. Our task is to trust. When we do come to know our call, its full implications will still exceed our grasp. The consequences will reach far beyond what we can foresee, even with the sharpest spiritual eyesight.

Like it or not, we are being led into an unknown land by the same divine mystery that beckons us to a journey of discovery. Each person's vocation remains unique and changing, as our grandfather-monk can readily testify.

Not to commit ourselves to fulfilling our call because we do not know its outcome would be a tragic mistake. Without faithfully following the lead of the Lord in our lives, we risk living a scattered, inconsistent, and ultimately disappointing existence. We become prisoners of the passing whims of our age. We find ourselves absorbed in functions that have lost their spark. The music of eternity fades so far into the background that it takes almost a tragedy for us to hear its refrain.

So accustomed are we to plodding along like robots without

inspiration that we forget what living the good life really means. Thomas à Kempis offers us this caution: "If you remain faithful and fervent in what you do, God will doubtless be faithful and generous in rewarding you. You must keep good hope of attaining the victory, but you must not become overconfident, lest you grow lazy or self-satisfied."[4]

Two points of clarity emerge from this wisdom: The bad news is that by not following a decisive disclosure of divine direction, it may or may not return. As a forger knows, the iron must be struck when it's hot. If we let the moment grow cold, we must accept the consequences. We all know the lament of the fellow who had the right girl but could not make up his mind to marry her.

The good news is that it is never too late to recommit ourselves to what God wants us to be and to do, even though this "what" always remains somewhat mysterious. If we could see and understand everything, of what use would faith be? If someone asked us in advance how pieces of the puzzle will fall into place, we would be hard-pressed for an answer. Who of us could penetrate such a wondrous mystery as this? All we can do is to abandon ourselves into God's guiding hand, appreciate our call, and follow its beckoning with as much fidelity as we can muster.

PRACTICING CALL-APPRECIATION

Our human understanding is too limited to grasp anything but one small step on the journey at a time. And we often need to take that next clear step before God will show us how to proceed from there. Rather than trying to analyze every detail of divine guidance, it is best to practice call-appreciation.

We can keep following the path to holiness in the conviction that God is guiding us firmly and gently, whether we know it or not. We can trust that the Holy Spirit never ceases to whisper his direction through the filter of seemingly unrelated incidents, choices, and events. These are the arena in which grace does its transforming work and leads us to call-fulfillment.

Trust in divine disclosures helps us to stay flexible, like clay in the potter's hands. We face a formidable challenge in responding to all the demands and details of our call without losing track of their deeper meaning. Daily happenings provide windows through which we can catch a glimpse of the mysterious love that directs our lives. We behold people, events, and things as pointers to that holy pattern. Beyond unknown dangers and fears lie paths not anticipated, new ways that will enable us to tune in to what is, to appreciate what has gone before, and to anticipate what is to come.

What keeps us from gaining ground and from striving fervently to fulfill our call? Thomas à Kempis gives this answer:

> Those people progress most in virtue—truly, they progress beyond all others—who make a valiant effort to overcome the things that are most troublesome to them, that work most against them. A person makes more progress and deserves fuller grace in those instances where he overcomes such obstacles completely and where he cleanses his spirit by doing so.
>
> ... When you come to this, that you look for your comfort from nothing but God, then you begin to know God perfectly; then, too, will you be quite content no matter what happens; then, you will neither rejoice for much nor grieve for little, but will commit yourself wholly and confidently to God, for he means everything to you. To God, nothing passes away or dies, but all things live and all things serve him promptly at a nod.[5]

This spiritual master is urging us to be faithful in little things, and to take comfort in the fact that along the way of divine guidance, nothing escapes God's loving glance. That is why in everything we do, in all that we are, we can serve him "promptly at a nod." At every point along our journey, let us pray in the spirit of *The Imitation of Christ*:

> *Lord, I believe in you, I hope in you, I love you. Give me a praying heart, and make of me a living prayer. Come into my life as my Savior, my Divine Guide, my Friend. In my need, let me spontaneously, in childlike trust, call on your name.*

*Give me the courage to act on faith even when I do not under-
stand what is happening to me or why. Let me know that you are a
God who hears my prayer, who heals me physically, spiritually, men-
tally, and emotionally. Lord, give me the grace to surrender myself
unconditionally to you. Amen.*

TIME TO REFLECT

Here is a final exercise to help you foster the art and discipline of
asking for and listening to the guidance of God. Spend some time
responding to the following five questions and doing the recommended readings from Scripture and the classics. If the opportunity
presents itself, you may wish to share your reflections and responses
with a spiritual guide or friend, a confidante, or a Christian faith
group.

1. Do I love God with my whole body, mind, heart, and soul?

    Scripture: Mark 12:28-34 ("Which is the first of all the com-
    mandments?"); Romans 12:9-11 ("Love one another with
    mutual affection").

    The Dialogue by Catherine of Siena, pp. 38-39 (How to serve
    your neighbors).

2. Do I show care, concern, and compassion for the people
    around me and others in need of my charitable outreach? Do I
    demonstrate love for others in my ministry?

    Scripture: 1 Corinthians 13:1-13 ("The greatest of these is
    love"); John 15:12-14 ("... to lay down one's life for one's
    friends").

    Story of a Soul by St. Thérèse of Lisieux, pp. 193-194 ("My
    vocation is love!").

3. Do I experience myself as God's work of art? Do I appreciate
    my gifts?

Scripture: 2 Timothy 4:1-8 ("Fulfill your ministry"); Romans 5:1-5 ("We have been justified by faith").

The Ascent of Mount Carmel by St. John of the Cross, pp. 115-116 ("I submit entirely to the church, the pure and reliable road leading to union").

4. Am I conscious of doing whatever I do in service of God? How am I helping to continue the work of transformation begun by Christ and extending to the present age?

   Scripture: Hebrews 3:4-14 ("Encourage yourself daily while it is still today, so that none of you may grow hardened by the deceit of sin"); 1 Peter 1:18-23 ("The living and abiding word of God").

   The Life of St. Francis by Bonaventure, pp. 179-82 (St. Francis preached the gospel of peace and salvation; he was an example for those who would be perfect followers of Christ).

5. Am I the same person in private as I am in public? Am I a living witness to the gospel wherever I go, whatever I do?

   Scripture: 1 Thessalonians 2:4-13 ("We were judged worthy by God to be entrusted with the gospel"); 1 Peter 3:13-17 "Be ready to give an explanation to anyone who asks you for a reason for your hope").

   Clare of Assisi, The Complete Works, p. 232 ("Constant perseverance to the end").

STILL DELIGHT IN DAILY DUTIES
Adrian van Kaam

I feel low in spirit, Lord.
Whisper a word
Of fidelity
That generates serenity
In my uncertain heart.
Make me the ward of your wish
To save my limping life.

My trust should be bold,
You told prophets of old,
People of Galilee,
Fishers in the boat
That crossed the sea,
Throwing out a net
In trust of you, instead
Of in their skill alone.

Help me to fulfill my call
On the mountain of fidelity
That holds humanity,
The dawning of its day,
The passing of each century.
Set me free as a bird in the sky,
A lily that blooms without why,
A wounded tree daily healed
By appreciation that yields
Fruits from starving branches.

Your love dances through dissonances
Of hearts that faint in pain,
Reviving once again
A still delight in daily duties
No longer meaningless and vain.

For my call is the coin
Lost and found by you alone,
Eternal seeker, ever trailing
High or deep the wailing sheep,
Guiding each one tenderly
Through the gate of your fidelity.

NOTES

ONE
The Mystery of Divine Guidance

1. See Susan Muto, *The Blessings that Make Us Be: A Formative Approach to Living the Beatitudes* (New York: Crossroad; reprinted Petersham, Mass.: St. Bede's, 1980), which treats the beatitudes as "modes of being" prompting "ways of acting" in Christ's name.
2. For an excellent contemporary treatment of the beatitudes as modes of social action and Christian presence, see Benedict Groeschel, *Heaven in Our Hands* (Ann Arbor, Mich.: Servant, 1994).

TWO
Diving Deeper

1. See Charles Colson, *Born Again* (Grand Rapids, Mich.: Baker, 1977) and *Life Sentence* (Grand Rapids, Mich.: Baker, 1981). For further information about the radical calling of the church to be the people of God, see also Charles Colson and Ellen Santilli Vaughn, *The Body* (Dallas, Tex.: Word, 1992).
2. Jean Pierre de Caussade, *The Sacrament of the Present Moment*, trans. Kitty Muggeridge (New York: Harper & Row, 1982), 42. See also Adrian van Kaam and Susan Muto, *Practicing the Prayer of Presence* (Williston Park, N.Y.: Resurrection, 1993).
3. de Caussade, 42.
4. de Caussade, 42.
5. de Caussade, 43.
6. See Brother Lawrence of the Resurrection, *The Practice of the Presence of God*, trans. Donald Attwater (Springfield, Ill.: Templegate, 1974).
7. Jean Pierre de Caussade, *Abandonment to Divine Providence*, trans. John Beevers (Garden City, N.Y.: Doubleday, 1975), 40.
8. de Caussade, *Abandonment*, 41.
9. de Caussade, *Abandonment*, 41.
10. de Caussade, *Abandonment*, 41.

THREE
Standing Still While Still Moving

1. Walter Ciszek with Daniel Flaherty, *He Leadeth Me* (Garden City, N.Y.: Doubleday, Image, 1973), 14.
2. Ciszek, 15.
3. Ciszek, 44.
4. See Susan Muto, *Meditation in Motion* (Garden City: Doubleday, 1986).
5. Ciszek, 44.
6. See Thomas Merton, *Contemplative Prayer* (New York: Herder and Herder, 1969).

FOUR
Repentance Opens Our Hearts to Hear God

1. Anonymous, *The Cloud of Unknowing,* James Walsh, S.J., Ed. *The Classics of Western Spirituality* (Ramsey, N.J.: Paulist, 1981), 55.
2. Irénée Hausheer, *Penthos: The Doctrine of Compunction in the Christian East,* trans. Anselm Hufstader (Kalamazoo, Mich.: Cistercian, 1982), 55.
3. St. Augustine, *The Confessions of St. Augustine,* trans. John K. Ryan, (New York: Doubleday, Image, 1960), 55.
4. Augustine, 274.
5. Augustine, 274.
6. Augustine, 275.
7. See Susan Muto, *John of the Cross for Today: The Ascent,* (Notre Dame: Ave Maria, 1991) and *John of the Cross for Today: The Dark Night* (Notre Dame: Ave Maria, 1994).

FIVE
Conversion of Heart Can Change the World

1. For a formative reading of this story, see Adrian van Kaam, *The Woman at the Well* (Reprinted Pittsburgh: Epiphany, 1993).
2. St. Thérèse of Lisieux, *The Story of a Soul: The Autobiography of St. Thérèse of Lisieux,* trans. John Clarke (Washington: ICS, 1975), 194.
3. Thérèse of Lisieux, 254.
4. Thérèse of Lisieux, 256.
5. Thérèse of Lisieux, 267.
6. See Teresa of Avila, *The Book of Her Life,* trans. Kieran Kavanaugh and Otilio Rodriguez, in *The Collected Works of St. Teresa of Avila,* Vol. I (Washington: ICS, 1976). This text makes clear why for St. Teresa "God alone suffices."
7. Thérèse of Lisieux, 195.
8. For further insights into the unique and communal meaning of conversion of heart, see Adrian van Kaam, *The Science of Formative Spirituality: Formation of the Human Heart,* Vol. III (New York: Crossroad, 1986).

SIX
Forgiveness Melts the Barriers to Grace

1. St. Teresa of Avila, *The Way of Perfection*, trans. Kieran Kavanaugh and Otilio Rodriguez, in *The Collected Works of St. Teresa of Avila*, Vol. II (Washington: ICS, 1980), 177.
2. Teresa of Avila, *The Way of Perfection*, 182.
3. Teresa of Avila, *The Way of Perfection*, 182.
4. Teresa of Avila, *The Way of Perfection*, 182.
5. Teresa of Avila, *The Way of Perfection*, 183.
6. Teresa of Avila, *The Way of Perfection*, 184.
7. Teresa of Avila, *The Way of Perfection*, 200-201.
8. Teresa of Avila, *The Way of Perfection*, 198.

SEVEN
Compassion: A God-Guided Gift

1. Donald McNeill, Douglas Morrison, and Henri J.M. Nouwen, *Compassion: A Reflection on the Christian Life* (Garden City, N.Y.: Doubleday, 1982), 45.
2. Thérèse of Lisieux, *The Story of a Soul*, 248-49.
3. Julian of Norwich, *Showings*, trans. Edmund Colledge and James Walsh, in *Classics of Western Spirituality* (Mahwah, N.J.: Paulist, 1978), 262.
4. Julian of Norwich, *Showings*, 263.
5. Julian of Norwich, *Showings*, 262.
6. Julian of Norwich, *Showings*, 262.

EIGHT
Meekness Keeps Our Hearts Teachable

1. Adrian van Kaam, *A Light to the Gentiles* (Pittsburgh: Duquesne University Press, 1959), 266-67.
2. Adrian van Kaam, *A Light to the Gentiles*, 267.
3. See Adrian van Kaam, *Spirituality and the Gentle Life* (Pittsburgh: Epiphany, 1994).
4. St. Francis de Sales, *Introduction to the Devout Life*, trans. John K. Ryan (Garden City: Doubleday, 1972), 149.
5. Francis de Sales, 151.
6. Francis de Sales, 146. See also *The Rule of St. Benedict*, ed. Timothy Fry (Collegeville, Minn.: Liturgical, 1981).
7. Francis de Sales, 146-147.
8. Francis de Sales, 149.
9. Teresa of Avila, *The Way of Perfection*, 165.

NINE
Peace Anchors Us in the Divine Family

1. Catherine of Siena, *The Dialogue*, trans. Suzanne Noffke, in *The Classics of Western Spirituality* (Mahwah, N.J.: Paulist, 1980), 163. See also *Peaceweavers: Medieval Religious Women*, Lillian Thomas Shank and John Nichols, eds. (Kalamazoo, Mich.: Cistercian, 1987).
2. Catherine of Siena, 163-164.
3. Catherine of Siena, 188.
4. Catherine of Siena, 159. See also *Peaceweavers*, 225.
5. Catherine of Siena, 189.
6. Catherine of Siena, 211.
7. See Thérèse of Lisieux, *The Story of a Soul*.
8. Catherine of Siena, 360.
9. See Adrian van Kaam and Susan Muto, *The Power of Appreciation: A New Approach to Personal and Relational Healing* (New York: Crossroad, 1992).

TEN
Poverty: Depending on God for Everything

1. *Francis and Clare, The Complete Works*, trans. Regis J Armstrong and Ignatius Brady, in *The Classics of Western Spirituality* (Mahwah, N.J.: Paulist, 1978), 32. See also Bonaventure, *The Soul's Journey into God: The Tree of Life; The Life of St. Francis*, trans. Ewart Cousins, in *The Classics of Western Spirituality* (New York: Paulist, 1978).
2. *Francis and Clare, The Complete Works*, 193.
3. *Francis and Clare, The Complete Works*, 193.
4. *Francis and Clare, The Complete Works*, 193.
5. *Francis and Clare, The Complete Works*, 193.
6. For a further analysis of the life call in relation to commitment and consecration, see Susan Muto and Adrian van Kaam, *Commitment: Key to Christian Maturity* (Mahwah, N.J.: Paulist, 1989), and *Commitment: Key to Christian Maturity: A Workbook and Study Guide* (Mahwah, N.J.: Paulist, 1991).

ELEVEN
Purity Opens Our Eyes of Faith

1. See Susan Muto, *Pathways of Spiritual Living* (New York: Doubleday, 1984), (Reprinted Petersham, Mass.: St. Bede's, 1988).
2. St. John of the Cross, *The Living Flame of Love*, in *The Collected Works of St. John of the Cross*, trans. Kieran Kavanaugh and Otilio Rodriguez (Washington: ICS, 1991), 422.

TWELVE
Responding to the Grace of Guidance

1. See Elizabeth of the Trinity, *The Complete Works*, Vol. I, trans. Aletheia Kane (Washington: ICS, 1984).
2. *The Cloud of Unknowing*, 185-86.
3. *The Cloud of Unknowing*, 185-86.
4. *The Cloud of Unknowing*, 208-209.
5. See Adrian van Kaam, *The Music of Eternity: Everyday Sound of Fidelity* (Notre Dame: Ave Maria, 1990).

THIRTEEN
Fulfilling Our Call

1. See Thomas Dubay, *Seeking Spiritual Direction: How to Grow the Divine Life Within* (Ann Arbor, Mich.: Servant, 1993).
2. See Adrian van Kaam, *The Mystery of Transforming Love* (Denville, N.J.: Dimension, 1982).
3. Thomas à Kempis, *The Imitation of Christ: A Timeless Classic for Contemporary Readers*, trans. William C. Creasy (Notre Dame: Ave Maria, 1989), 47.
4. Thomas à Kempis, 59.
5. Thomas à Kempis, 47.

BIBLIOGRAPHY

à Kempis, Thomas. *The Imitation of Christ: A Timeless Classic for Contemporary Readers.* Trans. William C. Creasy. Notre Dame: Ave Maria, 1989.

Anthony, Edd. *Jesus According to....* Boston: St. Paul, 1992.

Aquinas, Thomas. *Treatise on Happiness.* Trans. John A. Oesterle. Notre Dame: Univ. of Notre Dame Press, 1983.

Arndt, Johann. *True Christianity* in *Classics of Western Spirituality.* Trans. Peter Erb. Mahwah, N.J.: Paulist, 1979.

Augustine. *The Confessions.* Trans. John K. Ryan. Garden City, N.J.: Doubleday, 1960.

Bernard of Clairvaux: Selected Works in *The Classics of Western Spirituality.* Trans. G.R. Evans. New York: Paulist, 1987.

Beevers, John. *Storm of Glory: The Story of St. Thérèse of Lisieux.* Garden City, N.Y.: Doubleday, Image, 1955.

Bobo, Murray. *Tales of St. Francis.* Cincinnati: St. Anthony Messenger, 1992.

Bonaventure: The Soul's Journey into God; The Tree of Life; The Life of St. Francis in *The Classics of Western Spirituality.* Trans. Ewart Cousins. New York: Paulist, 1978.

Bonhoeffer, Dietrich. *Meditating on the Word.* Trans. David Gracie. Cambridge, Mass.: Cowley, 1986.

Boucher, John J. *Is Talking to God a Long Distance Call?* Ann Arbor, Mich.: Servant, 1990.

Bouyer, Louis. *Women Mystics.* San Francisco: Ignatius, 1993.

Catherine of Siena. *The Dialogue* in *The Classics of Western Spirituality*. Trans. Suzanne Noffke. New York: Paulist, 1980.

Ciszek, Walter J., with Daniel Flaherty. *He Leadeth Me*. Garden City, N.Y.: Doubleday, Image, 1975.

Cloud of Unknowing, The. James Walsh, ed. New York: Paulist, 1981.

Colson, Charles. *Born Again*. Grand Rapids: Baker, 1977.

___. *Life Sentence*. Grand Rapids: Baker, 1981.

Colson, Charles with Ellen Santilli Vaughn. *The Body*. Dallas: Word, 1992.

Crosby, Michael H. *Spirituality of the Beatitudes: Matthew's Challenge for First World Christians*. Maryknoll, N.J.: Orbis, 1981.

Day, Albert Edward. *Discipline and Discovery*. Workbook Ed. Nashville: The Upper Room, 1977.

de Caussade, Jean-Pierre. *Abandonment to Divine Providence*. Trans. John Beevers. Garden City, N.Y.: Doubleday, 1975.

___. *The Sacrament of the Present Moment*. Trans. Kitty Muggeridge. New York: Harper & Row, 1982.

de Sales, Francis. *Introduction to the Devout Life*. Trans. John K. Ryan. rev. ed. New York: Image, Doubleday, 1972.

DeSiano, Frank, and Kenneth Boyack. *Discovering My Experience of God: Awareness and Witness*. Mahwah, N.J.: Paulist, 1992.

Dubay, Thomas. *Seeking Spiritual Direction: How to Grow the Divine Life Within*. Ann Arbor, Mich.: Servant, 1993.

Dunnam, Maxie. *The Workbook on Spiritual Disciplines*. Nashville: The Upper Room, 1984.

Elizabeth of the Trinity. *The Complete Works*, Vol. I. Trans. Sr. Aletheia Kane. Washington: ICS, 1984.

___. *Light Love Life*. Washington: ICS, 1984.

Fesch, Jacques. *Light Upon the Scaffold*. Trans. Matthew J. O'Connell. St. Meinrad, Ind.: Abbey, 1975.

Foster, Richard J. *Celebration of Discipline: The Path to Spiritual Growth.* San Francisco: Harper & Row, 1978.

Francis and Clare: The Collected Works in *The Classics of Western Spirituality.* Trans. Regis J. Armstrong and Ignatius C. Brady. New York: Paulist, 1982.

Francis of Assisi. *Writings and Early Biographies.* Marion A. Habig, ed. Chicago: Franciscan Herald, 1973.

Gertrude of Helfta: The Herald of Divine Love in *The Classics of Western Spirituality.* New York: Paulist, 1993.

Gilbert, Alphonse. *You Have Laid Your Hand on Me...* Rome: Spiritan Research and Animation Centre, 1983.

Gratton, Carolyn. *The Art of Spiritual Guidance.* New York: Crossroad, 1992.

Groeschel, Benedict. *Heaven in Our Hands.* Ann Arbor, Mich.: Servant, 1994.

Guigo II. *The Ladder of Monks and Twelve Meditations.* Trans. Edmund Colledge. Kalamazoo, Mich.: Cistercian, 1981.

Hausherr, Irénée. *Penthos: The Doctrine of Compunction in the Christian East.* Trans. Anselm Hufstader. Kalamazoo, Mich.: Cistercian, 1982.

Hilton, Walter. *The Stairway of Perfection.* Trans. M.L. Del Mastro. Garden City, N.Y.: Image, Doubleday, 1979.

Ignatius of Loyola. *Notes on the Spiritual Exercises.* St. Louis: Review for Religious, 1981.

Ignatius of Loyola: The Spiritual Exercises and Selected Works in *The Classics of Western Spirituality.* New York: Paulist, 1991.

Jamart, Francois. *Complete Spiritual Doctrine of St. Thérèse of Lisieux.* Trans. Walter van de Putte. New York: Alba, 1961.

John of the Cross. *The Collected Works.* Trans. Kieran Kavanaugh and Otilio Rodriguez. Washington: ICS, 1991.

Julian of Norwich: Showings in *The Classics of Western Spirituality.* New York: Paulist, 1978.

Kelly, Thomas R. *A Testament of Devotion.* New York: Harper & Row, 1941.

Lawrence, Brother, of the Resurrection. *The Practice of the Presence of God*. Trans. Donald Attwater. Springfield, Ill.: Templegate, 1974.

McNeill, Donald P., Douglas A. Morrison, Henri J. M. Nouwen. *Compassion: A Reflection on the Christian Life*. Garden City, N.Y.: Doubleday, 1982.

Merton, Thomas. *Contemplative Prayer*. New York: Herder and Herder, 1969.

Mulholland, M. Robert, Jr. *Invitation to a Journey*. Downers Grove, Ill.: InterVarsity Press, 1993.

Muto, Susan. *Blessings that Make Us Be: A Formative Approach to Living the Beatitudes*. New York: Crossroad; Reprinted Petersham, Mass.: St. Bede's, 1980.

___. *John of the Cross for Today: The Ascent*. Notre Dame: Ave Maria, 1991.

___. *John of the Cross for Today: The Dark Night*. Notre Dame: Ave Maria, 1994.

___. *Meditation in Motion*. New York: Doubleday, 1986.

___. *Pathways of Spiritual Living*. New York: Doubleday; Reprinted Petersham, Mass.: St. Bede's, 1988.

Muto, Susan and Adrian van Kaam. *Commitment: Key to Christian Maturity*. New York: Paulist, 1989.

___. *Commitment: Key to Christian Maturity: A Workbook and Study Guide*. Mahwah, N.J.: Paulist, 1991.

Peaceweavers: Medieval Religious Women. Vol. II. Lillian Thomas and John Nichols, eds. Kalamazoo, Mich.: Cistercian, 1987.

Puls, Joan. *A Spirituality of Compassion*. Mystic, Conn.: Twenty-Third, 1988.

___. *Every Bush Is Burning*. Mystic, Conn.: Twenty-Third, 1985.

Ramey, Robert H., Jr. and Ben Campbell Johnson. *Living the Christian Life: A Guide to Reformed Spirituality*. Louisville: Westminster/John Knox, 1992.

Rolle, Richard. *The Fire of Love and the Mending of Life*. Garden City, N.Y.: Doubleday, Image, 1981.

Rule of St. Benedict, The. Timothy Fry, ed. Collegeville, Minn.: 1981.

Schuller, Robert H. *The Be Happy Attitudes*. New York: Bantam, 1987.

Stein, Edith. *On the Problem of Empathy.* Third Rev. Ed. Washington: ICS, 1989.

Storr, Anthony. *Solitude: A Return to the Self.* New York: Ballantine, 1988.

Tauler, Johann. *Spiritual Conferences.* Trans. Eric Colledge and Sr. M. Jane. Rockford, Ill.: Tan, 1978.

Teresa of Avila. *The Way of Perfection* in *The Collected Works.* Vol. 1. Trans. Kieran Kavanaugh and Otilio Rodriguez, Second Rev. Ed. Washington: ICS, 1980.

____. *The Collected Works,* Vol. 2. Trans. Kieran Kavanaugh and Otilio Rodriguez. Washington: ICS, 1980.

Thérèse of Lisieux. *Story of a Soul.* Trans. John Clarke. Washington: ICS, 1975.

Tracy, Wesley D., E. Dee Freeborn, Janine Tartaglia, Morris A. Weigelt. *The Upward Call: Spiritual Formation and the Holy Life.* Kansas City, Mo.: Beacon Hill, 1994.

van Kaam, Adrian. *A Light to the Gentiles.* Pittsburgh: Duquesne Univ. Press, 1959.

____. *Dynamics of Spiritual Self Direction.* Pittsburgh: Epiphany Association, 1992.

____. *Looking for Jesus.* Denville, N.J.: Dimension, 1978.

____. *The Music of Eternity: Everyday Sound of Fidelity.* Notre Dame: Ave Maria, 1990.

____. *The Mystery of Transforming Love.* Denville, N.J.: Dimension, 1982.

____. *The Science of Formative Spirituality.* Vol. 3, Formation of the Human Heart. New York: Crossroad, 1986.

____. *Spirituality and the Gentle Life.* Pittsburgh: Epiphany, 1994.

____. *The Woman at the Well.* Denville, N. J.: Dimension, reprinted Pittsburgh: Epiphany, 1993.

van Kaam, Adrian and Susan Muto. *The Power of Appreciation: A New Approach to Personal and Relational Healing.* New York: Crossroad, 1992.

____. *Practicing the Prayer of Presence.* Williston Park, N.Y.: Resurrection, 1993.

van Ruysbroek, Jan. *Spiritual Espousals.* Trans. Eric Colledge. Westminster, Md.: Christian Classics, 1983.

Vaught, Carl G. *The Sermon on the Mount: A Theological Interpretation.* Albany, N.Y.: State University of New York Press, 1986.

Vest, Norvene. *Bible Reading for Spiritual Growth.* San Francisco: Harper San Francisco, 1993.

von Balthasar, Hans Urs. *Two Sisters in the Spirit: Thérèse of Lisieux and Elizabeth of the Trinity.* San Francisco: Ignatius, 1992.

The Way of a Pilgrim and *The Pilgrim Continues His Way.* Trans. R.M. French. New York: Seabury, 1968.

Webster, Douglas D. *Finding Spiritual Direction.* Downers Grove, Ill.: InterVarsity Press, 1991.

Wojtyla, Karol. *Faith According to Saint John of the Cross.* Trans. Jordan Aumann. San Francisco: Ignatius, 1981.

Wright, Wendy M. *Bond of Perfection: Jeanne de Chantal and Francois de Sales.* New York: Paulist, 1985.

Author's note: All books by Susan Muto and Adrian van Kaam can be obtained by writing to the Epiphany Association, 1145 Beechwood Boulevard, Pittsburgh, PA 15206. 412-661-5678 (phone), and 412- 661-3536 (fax).

INDEX OF POEMS BY TITLE AND FIRST LINE

Poems by Father Adrian van Kaam

Other Books of Interest from Servant Publications

Heaven in Our Hands
by Father Benedict Groeschel

Father Benedict Groeschel believes that far too many Christians have lost touch with how revolutionary the Beatitudes are in today's world, where it seems that it is always the rich and powerful who reap all the rewards. In these provocative reflections on the Sermon on the Mount, Father Groeschel shows us how the Beatitudes reveal to us the very heart of God, giving us the blessings we long for—now and in eternity. **$8.99**

Beginning Spiritual Direction
by Msgr. David E. Rosage

Drawing upon many years of experience as a spiritual director, Monsignor David E. Rosage shows you how to begin a spiritual journey that will lead to a deeper personal relationship with God and a clearer understanding of his will. **$7.99**

Available at your Christian bookstore or from:
Servant Publications • Dept. 209 • P.O. Box 7455
Ann Arbor, Michigan 48107
Please include payment plus $2.75 per book
for postage and handling.
*Send for our FREE catalog of Christian
books, music, and cassettes.*